W9-BYS-238

Anton Szandor LaVey

Called "The Black Pope" by many of his followers, Anton LaVey began the road to High Priesthood of the Church of Satan when he was only 16 years old and an organ player in a carnival:

"On Saturday night I would see men lusting after half-naked girls dancing at the carnival, and on Sunday morning when I was playing the organ for tent-show evangelists at the other end of the carnival lot, I would see these same men sitting in the pews with their wives and children, asking God to forgive them and purge them of carnal desires. And the next Saturday night they'd be back at the carnival or some other place of indulgence.

"I knew then that the Christian Church thrives on hypocrisy, and that man's carnal nature will out!"

From that time early in his life his path was clear. Finally, on the last night of April, 1966—*Walpurgisnacht,* the most important festival of the believers in witchcraft—LaVey shaved his head in the tradition of ancient executioners and announced the formation of The Church Of Satan. He had seen the need for a church that would recapture man's body and his carnal desires as objects of celebration. *"Since worship of fleshly things produces pleasure,"* he said, *"there would then be a temple of glorious indulgence . . ."*

Other Avon Books by
Anton Szandor LaVey

THE SATANIC RITUALS

ATTENTION: ORGANIZATIONS AND CORPORATIONS
Most Avon Books paperbacks are available at special quantity discounts for bulk purchases for sales promotions, premiums, or fund-raising. For information, please call or write:

**Special Markets Department, HarperCollins Publishers Inc.
10 East 53rd Street, New York, New York 10022-5299.
Telephone: (212) 207-7528. Fax: (212) 207-7222.**

The Satanic Bible

Anton Szandor LaVey

AVON BOOKS

An Imprint of HarperCollinsPublishers

AVON BOOKS
An Imprint of HarperCollins*Publishers*
195 Broadway,
New York, NY 10007

Copyright © 1969 by Anton Szandor LaVey
Introduction copyright © 2005 by Magus Peter H. Gilmore
ISBN: 0-380-01539-0
www.avonbooks.com

All rights reserved. No part of this book may be used or reproduced in any manner whatsoever without written permission, except in the case of brief quotations embodied in critical articles and reviews. For information address Avon Books, an imprint of HarperCollins Publishers.

First Avon Books paperback printing: December 1969

Avon Trademark Reg. U.S. Pat. Off. and in Other Countries, Marca Registrada, Hecho en U.S.A.
HarperCollins® is a trademark of HarperCollins Publishers Inc.

Printed in the U.S.A.

111

If you purchased this book without a cover, you should be aware that this book is stolen property. It was reported as "unsold and destroyed" to the publisher, and neither the author nor the publisher has received any payment for this "stripped book."

For Diane

OPENING THE ADAMANTINE GATES

An Introduction to *The Satanic Bible*
by Magus Peter H. Gilmore

This book has the potential to change your life—it did mine. It is a diabolical work, written with elegance, earthiness, and might, serving quite magically as a mirror. If you look within these pages and see yourself; if you find its principles to be those you've lived by as long as you can remember; if you feel the evocation of an overwhelming sense of homecoming, then you will have discovered that you are a part of a scattered "meta-tribe," and the proper name for what you are is "Satanist."

I first encountered Anton Szandor LaVey through *The Satanic Bible*, at the age of thirteen when I was an avowed atheist. Not being partial to literature promoting faith of any sort, I was pleasantly surprised that this was no rant by someone claiming direct contact with Satan. Instead, I found a common sense, rational, materialist philosophy, along with theatrical ritual techniques meant as self-transformative psychodrama. Here was a tool perfectly suited to my nature as a means for getting the most out of my life. I knew that "atheist" was no longer sufficient as a designation for myself. This book lead me to meet and befriend LaVey, working with him to administer the Church he created, and finally to succeed him as the second High Priest of the Church of Satan.

It is one of Anton LaVey's numerous talents that his written words are vivid, brimming with his distinct personality. His well-wrought phrases give the sense of encountering the man himself, and such an impression is not a delusion. When my wife, Peggy Nadramia, and I met "The Doctor" (an affectionate moniker used by those close to him), we agreed that here was exactly the man we had dared to expect from reading his books.

Unlike the founders of other religions who claimed exalted "inspiration" delivered through some supernatural entity, LaVey readily acknowledged that he used his own faculties to synthesize Satanism. He based it on both his understanding of the human animal acquired from life experience and the wisdom he'd gained from other advocates of materialism, pragmatism, and individualism. His blasphemously named "Church of Satan" was consciously designed to be an adversary to existing "spiritual" belief systems. It was the first organization promulgating a religious philosophy championing Satan as the symbol of liberty and individualism. Concerning his role as founder, he said that, "If he didn't do it himself, someone else, perhaps less qualified, would have." His perceptive insights thus lead him to give a proper name to a human type that has always been part of our species.

LaVey was born in Chicago in 1930, and his parents soon relocated to California, that westernmost gathering place for the brightest and darkest manifestations of the "American Dream." It was a fertile environment for the sensitive child who would eventually mature into a role that the press would dub "The Black Pope." From his Eastern European grandmother, young LaVey learned of the superstitions that are still extant in that part of the world. These tales whetted his appetite for the outré, leading him to become absorbed in classic dark literature such as *Dracula* and *Frankenstein*. He also became an avid reader of the pulp magazines, which first published tales now deemed classics of the horror and science fiction genres. He later befriended seminal *Weird Tales* authors such as Clark Ashton Smith, Robert Barbour Johnson, and George Hass. His fancy was captured by fictional characters found in the works of Jack London and Somerset Maugham, in comic strip characters like Ming the Merciless, as well as by historical figures of a diabolical cast such as Cagliostro, Rasputin, and Basil Zaharoff. More interesting to him than the available occult literature, which he dismissed as being little more than sanctimonious white magic, were books of applied obscure knowledge such as Dr. William Wesley Cook's *Practical Lessons in Hypnotism, Jane's Fighting Ships*, and manuals for handwriting analysis.

His musical abilities were noticed early, and he was given free reign by his parents to try his hand at various instruments. LaVey was mainly attracted to the keyboards because of their scope and versatility. He found time to practice and could easily reproduce songs heard by ear without recourse to fake books or sheet music. This talent would prove to be one of his main sources of income for many years, particularly his calliope playing during his carnival days, and later his many stints as an organist in bars, lounges, and nightclubs. These venues gave him the chance to study how various melodic lines and chord progressions swayed the emotions of his audiences, from the spectators at the carnival and spook shows to the individuals seeking solace for the disappointments in their lives in distilled spirits and the smoke-filled taverns for which LaVey's playing provided a moody soundtrack.

His odd interests marked him as an outsider, and he did not alleviate this by feeling any compulsion to be "one of the boys." He despised gym class and team sports and often cut classes to follow his own interests. Moving beyond the standard school texts, he absorbed volumes analyzing human behavior on every level, from the impulses of the individual to the dynamics of the herd. He watched films that would later be labeled *film noir* as well as German expressionist cinema such as *M*, *The Cabinet of Dr. Caligari*, and the *Dr. Mabuse* movies. His taste for flashy apparel also served to amplify his alienation from the mainstream.

He dropped out of high school to hang around with hoodlum types and gravitated towards working in the circus and carnivals, first as a roustabout and cage boy and later as a musician. His always-active curiosity was rewarded as he "learned the ropes" from the carnies. He worked an act with the big cats—he had an affinity for these powerful predators—and later assisted with the machinations of the spook shows. He became well-versed in the many rackets used to separate the rubes from their money, along with the psychology that lead people to such pursuits. Under the name "The Great Szandor" he played calliope and organ for the bawdy shows on Saturday nights, as well as for tent revivalists on Sunday mornings, seeing many of the same men attending both and noting this telling contradiction. All of these activities provided a firm, earthy background for his evolving cynical worldview.

When the carnival season ended, LaVey would earn money by playing organ in Los Angeles area burlesque houses, and he relates that it was during this period that he met and had a brief affair with a then-unknown Marilyn Monroe, after accompanying her "chain-dragging" striptease at the Mayan Burlesque Theater. Moving back to San Francisco, LaVey worked for a while as a photographer for the police department, and, during the Korean War, enrolled in San Francisco City College as a criminology major to avoid the draft. Both his studies and occupation revealed grim insights into human nature and confirmed his rejection of spiritual doctrines. At this time he met and married Carole Lansing, who bore him his first daughter, Karla Maritza, in 1952. A few years earlier LaVey had examined the writings of Aleister Crowley, so in 1951 he decided to meet some of the Berkeley Thelemites. He was unimpressed, as they were more mystical and less "wicked" than he supposed they should be for disciples of Crowley's libertine creed.

During the 1950s, LaVey supplemented his income as an investigator of alleged supernatural phenomena, handling "nut calls" referred to him by friends in the police department. These experiences proved to him that many people were inclined to seek a bizarre, "otherworldly" explanation for phenomena that had prosaic causes. His rational explanations often disappointed the complainants, so LaVey invented exotic sources to make them feel better, giving him insight as to how belief functions in people's lives.

In 1956 he purchased a Victorian house on California Street in San Francisco's Richmond District. It was reputed to have been a speakeasy, and was tricked out with secret passages, possibly to aid in clandestine carnal activities. He painted it black, thus creating a haunted intrusion on an otherwise typical block, matching his own unique presence. It was only natural that it would later become home to the Church of Satan. After his death, the building remained unoccupied, a brooding "shunned house," until it was demolished on October 17 of 2001 by the real estate company that owned the property.

LaVey met and became entranced by Diane Hegarty in 1959; he then left Carole in 1960. Hegarty and LaVey never married, but she bore him his second daughter, Zeena Galatea in 1964 and was his companion for many years. Hegarty and LaVey later separated; she sued him for palimony and this was settled out of court.

Through his "ghost busting," and his frequent public gigs as an organist, including playing the Wurlitzer at the Lost Weekend cocktail lounge, LaVey became a local celebrity and his holiday parties attracted many San Francisco notables. Guests included Carin de Plessin, called "the Baroness" as she had grown up in the royal palace of Denmark, anthropologist Michael Harner, Chester A. Arthur III (grandson to the U.S. President), Forrest J. Ackerman (later, the publisher of *Famous Monsters of Filmland* and acknowledged expert on science fiction), author Fritz Leiber, local eccentric Dr. Cecil E. Nixon (creator of the musical automaton Isis), and underground filmmaker Kenneth Anger. From this crowd LaVey distilled what he called a "Magic Circle" of associates who shared his interest in the bizarre, the hidden side of what moves the world. As his expertise grew, LaVey began presenting Friday night lectures summarizing the fruits of his research. In 1965, LaVey was featured on the "The Brother Buzz Show", a humorous children's program hosted by marionettes. The focus was on LaVey's "Addams Family" lifestyle—making a living as a hypnotist, investigator of the paranormal, and organist, as well as on his highly unusual pet Togare, a Nubian lion.

In the process of creating his lectures, LaVey noticed many common threads, which he then began weaving into a tenebrous conceptual tapestry. When a member of his Magic Circle suggested that he had the basis for a new religion, LaVey agreed and decided to found the Church of Satan as the best means for communicating his ideas. And so, in 1966 on the night of May Eve—the traditional Witches' Sabbath—LaVey declared the founding of the Church of Satan and renumbered 1966 as the year One, *Anno Satanas*— the first year of the Age of Satan.

The attention of the press soon followed, particularly with the wedding of Radical journalist John Raymond to New York socialite Judith Case on February 1st, 1967. Famed photographer Joe Rosenthal was sent by the *San

Francisco Chronicle to capture an image that went onward to the pages of the *Los Angeles Times* and other prominent newspapers. LaVey began the mass dissemination of his philosophy via the release of a record album, *The Satanic Mass* (Murgenstrumm, 1968). The album featured a cover graphic named by LaVey as the "Sigil of Baphomet": the goat head in a pentagram, circled with the Hebrew word "Leviathan," which has since become the ubiquitous symbol of Satanism. Featured on the album was part of the rite of baptism written for three-year-old Zeena (performed on May 23rd, 1967). In addition to the actual recording of a Satanic ritual, side two of the LP had LaVey reading excerpts from the as-yet-unpublished *The Satanic Bible* over music by Beethoven, Wagner, and Sousa. His Friday lectures continued and he instituted a series of "Witches' Workshops" to instruct women in the art of attaining their will through glamour, feminine wiles, and the skillful discovery and exploitation of men's fetishes.

By the end of 1969, LaVey had taken monographs he had written to explain the philosophy and ritual practices of the Church of Satan and expanded them. His influences included philosophers such as Ayn Rand, Nietzsche, and Mencken, the base wisdom of the carnival folk, the observations of P.T. Barnum, and finally the imagery of the archfiend found in Twain, Milton, Byron, and other romantics. He prefaced these essays and rites with reworked excerpts from Ragnar Redbeard's *Might is Right* and concluded it with "Satanized" versions of John Dee's Enochian Keys to create *The Satanic Bible*. It has never gone out of print and remains the main source for the contemporary Satanic movement.

The philosophy presented in it is an integrated whole, not a smorgasbord from which one can pick and choose. It is meant only for a select few who are epicurean, pragmatic, worldly, atheistic, fiercely individualistic, materialistic, rational, and darkly poetic. There may be fellow travelers—atheists, misanthropes, humanists, freethinkers—who see only a partial reflection of themselves in this showstone. Satanism may thus attract these types in some ways, but ultimately it is not for them. If it was only a philosophy, such individualists might be welcome; it is more. Satanism moves into the realm of religion by having an aesthetic component, a system of symbolism, metaphor, and ritual in which Satan is embraced not as some Devil to be worshipped, but as a symbolic external projection of the highest potential of each individual Satanist. The identification Satanists have with Satan is an intentional barrier against those who cannot resonate with this sinister archetype.

The Satanic Bible was followed in 1971 by *The Compleat Witch* (re-released in 1989 as *The Satanic Witch*), a manual that teaches "Lesser Magic"—the ways and means of reading and manipulating people and their actions toward the fulfillment of one's desired goals. *The Satanic Rituals* (1972) was printed as a companion volume to *The Satanic Bible* and contains "Greater Magic" rituals culled from a Satanic tradition identified by LaVey in various world cultures. Two collections of essays, which range from the humorous and insightful to the gleefully sordid, *The Devil's Notebook* (1992) and *Satan Speaks* (1998), complete his written canon.

Since its founding, LaVey's Church of Satan attracted many varied people who shared an alienation from conventional religions, including celebrities Jayne Mansfield and Sammy Davis Jr., as well as rock stars King Diamond, Marilyn Manson, and Marc Almond who all became, at least for a time, card-carrying members. He numbered among his associates Robert Fuest, director of the Vincent Price "Dr. Phibes" films as well as *The Devil's Rain*; Jacques Vallee, ufologist and computer scientist, who was used as the basis for the character Lacombe, played by François Truffaut, in Spielberg's *Close Encounters of the Third Kind*; and Aime Michel known as a spelunker and publisher of *Morning of the Magicians*.

LaVey's influence spread through articles in the news media throughout the world, popular magazines such as *Look*, *McCalls*, *Argosy*, *Newsweek*, *Time*, and later *Seconds*, *The Nose*, and *Rolling Stone*, numerous men's magazines, and via talk shows such as Joe Pyne, Phil Donahue, and Johnny Carson. This publicity left a mark on novels like *Rosemary's Baby* (completed by Ira Levin during the early days of the Church's high profile media blitz) and Leiber's *Our Lady of Darkness*, and films such as *Rosemary's Baby* (1968), *The Devil's Rain* (1975), *The Car* (1977), *Dr. Dracula* (1980), and many of the "Devil Cult" films from the 1970s through today that picked up on symbolism from LaVey's writings. A feature length documentary, *Satanis: The Devil's Mass* (1969) covered the rituals and philosophy of the Church, while LaVey himself was profiled in Nick Bougas' 1993 video documentary *Speak of the Devil*.

The Doctor's musicianship is preserved on several recordings, primarily *Strange Music* (1994) and *Satan Takes a Holiday* (1995). These reflect his penchant for tunes from the 1930s through the 1950s, which range from humorous to doom-laden as well as devil-themed songs. LaVey renders them on a series of self-programmed synthesizers, imitating various instrumental groups. They are impressive, as these are not multi-track recordings, but are done in one take with the sounds of the full instrumental ensemble created through the simultaneous use of numerous synthesizers played by LaVey's dexterous fingers as well as his feet on an organ-style foot pedal keyboard hooked-up via midi.

While his relationship with Diane Hegarty crumbled in the late 70s, a new lady would enter his life to become his final companion. Blanche Barton became his helpmate, co-conspirator, High Priestess, lover, and best friend. She bore him his only son, Satan Xerxes Carnacki LaVey on November 1, 1993. As his health deteriorated in the mid-90s, LaVey preferred to spend time only with the people whom he found enriching, gaining him a reputation as a recluse. He died on October 29, 1997, of complications arising from heart disease. There was no deathbed repentance. He went proudly as he lived, as a Satanist, his only regrets being that he was leaving the great party that was life, and that he would miss seeing his young son Xerxes grow to manhood.

According to LaVey's wishes, Barton succeeded him as the head of the Church after his death. In 2001, she passed on this position to myself, Peter H. Gilmore, by then a longtime church administrator and member of the Council of Nine. In 2002, Magistra Barton exchanged her position as High Priestess with my wife Magistra Peggy Nadramia, another veteran administrator who was serving as chair of the Council of Nine.

Two biographies have been written about LaVey: *The Devil's Avenger* (1974) by Burton Wolfe and *Secret Life of a Satanist* (1990) by Blanche Barton. In recent years detractors of LaVey with rather obvious agendas have disputed the authenticity of some of the events chronicled in these books. They accuse him of fabrication and self-promotional exaggeration. LaVey was a skilled showman, a talent he never denied. However, the incidents detailed in both biographies that can be authenticated via photographic, testimonial, and documentary evidence far outweigh the items in dispute. The fact remains that LaVey pursued a course that exposed him to unusual individuals from all strata of society. It climaxed with his founding of the Church of Satan, which lead to international notoriety. He was gifted beyond what is normally considered a standard for excellence, turning his hand to many arts with a deftness usually gained through dedication to only one muse. He lived his life as a true exemplar of all that he extolled— pursuing his pleasures without stinting while producing works only attained through vigorous self-discipline.

LaVey succeeded in avoiding the fate of Mrs. Cassan, a character from Charles G. Finney's *The Circus of Dr. Lao*, a favored novel of The Doctor. Her doom was to die and be forgotten, for her life produced nothing that was memorable in either a creative or destructive manner. With his thoughts, now presented in multiple languages, continuing to inspire like minds around the globe, Anton Szandor LaVey has won a place in the arena of philosophical and religious discourse. We Satanists owe him our gratitude for symbolically opening the adamantine gates of Hell, by giving form and structure to a philosophy that names us as the Gods of our own subjective universes. His ultimate heresy against the complacent masses was to reject their idolized dictum that all men are equal. Consequently he challenged his comrades to exercise their faculties to judge and be judged in all that they do. He dethroned the seeking of external saviors and championed responsibility for all of one's actions and the resultant consequences. That is perhaps the most frightening principle to a society wherein none are held accountable for their behavior.

The Church of Satan remains a world-spanning cabal of those who work to continue human society's momentum along the vector set by LaVey. It shall remain the treasured domain of an imperious few, who live by their own blood and brains, who proudly reject any "good guy badge" and embrace the title of Satanist.

There is nothing to fear in *The Satanic Bible*, for it will not transform you into something that you are not. It cannot convert you, or persuade you in directions not inherent in your nature. Its power lies in its ability to show you what you are through your reaction to its contents. Embrace them, and your life shall gain a new focus, for you will have sharpened your understanding of your self, and you will see more clearly how you differ from those around you. Reject some or all of these hardnosed postulates, and you are free to move on towards whatever other spiritual or conceptual haven that provides you with satisfaction. However, you will no longer be ignorant of what it means to be a Satanist. If you've grasped these fundamentals and have the talent to read people, you might notice that there are such individuals about you, and like LaVey himself, that they are some of the most just and fascinating folks you'll have the pleasure of knowing.

Magus Peter H. Gilmore
High Priest, Church of Satan

The Satanic Bible

PREFACE

This book was written because, with very few exceptions, every tract and paper, every "secret" grimoire, all the "great works" on the subject of magic, are nothing more than sanctimonious fraud—guilt-ridden ramblings and esoteric gibberish by chroniclers of magical lore unable or unwilling to present an objective view of the subject. Writer after writer, in efforts to state the principles of "white and black magic," has succeeded instead in clouding the entire issue so badly that the would-be student of sorcery winds up stupidly pushing a planchette over a Ouija board, standing inside a pentagram waiting for a demon to present itself, limply tossing I-Ching yarrow stalks like so many stale pretzels, shuffling pasteboards to foretell a future which has lost any meaning, attending seminars guaranteed to flatten his ego—while doing the same to his wallet—and in general making a blithering fool of himself in the eyes of those who *know!*

The true magus knows that occult bookshelves abound with the brittle relics of frightened minds and sterile bodies, metaphysical journals of self-deceit, and constipated rule-books of Eastern mysticism. Far too long has the subject of Satanic magic and philosophy been written down by wild-eyed journalists of the right-hand path.

The old literature is the by-product of brains festering with fear and defeat, written unknowingly for the assistance of those who really rule the earth, and who, from their Hellish thrones, laugh with noisome mirth.

The flames of Hell burn brighter for the kindling supplied by these volumes of hoary misinformation and false prophecy.

Herein you will find truth—and fantasy. Each is necessary

for the other to exist; but each must be recognized for what it is. What you see may not always please you; but you *will see!*

Here is Satanic thought from a truly Satanic point of view.

Anton Szandor LaVey

The Church of Satan
San Francisco, Walpurgisnacht 1968

PROLOGUE

The gods of the right-hand path have bickered and quarreled for an entire age of earth. Each of these deities and their respective priests and ministers have attempted to find wisdom in their own lies. The ice age of religious thought can last but a limited time in this great scheme of human existence. The gods of wisdom-defiled have had their saga, and their millennium hath become as reality. Each, with his own "divine" path to paradise, hath accused the other of heresies and spiritual indiscretions. The Ring of the Nibelungen doth carry an everlasting curse, but only because those who seek it think in terms of "Good" and "Evil"—themselves being at all times "Good." The gods of the past have become as their own devils in order to live. Feebly, their ministers play the devil's game to fill their tabernacles and pay the mortgages on their temples. Alas, too long have they studied "righteousness," and poor and incompetent devils they make. So they all join hands in "brotherly" unity, and in their desperation go to Valhalla for their last great ecumenical council. "Draweth near in the gloom the twilight of the gods." The ravens of night have flown forth to summon Loki, who hath set Valhalla aflame with the searing trident of the Inferno. The twilight is done. A glow of new light is borne out of the night and Lucifer is risen, once more to proclaim: "This is the age of Satan! Satan Rules the Earth!" The gods of the unjust are dead. This is the morning of magic, and undefiled wisdom. The FLESH prevaileth and a great Church shall be builded, consecrated in its name. No longer shall man's

23

salvation be dependent on his self-denial. And it will be known that the world of the flesh and the living shall be the greatest preparation for any and all eternal delights!

REGIE SATANAS!

AVE SATANAS!

HAIL SATAN!

THE NINE SATANIC STATEMENTS

1   Satan represents indulgence, instead of abstinence!

2   Satan represents vital existence, instead of spiritual pipe dreams!

3   Satan represents undefiled wisdom, instead of hypocritical self-deceit!

4   Satan represents kindness to those who deserve it, instead of love wasted on ingrates!

5   Satan represents vengeance, instead of turning the other cheek!

6   Satan represents responsibility to the responsible, instead of concern for psychic vampires!

7   Satan represents man as just another animal, sometimes better, more often worse than those that walk on all-fours, who, because of his "divine spiritual and intellectual development," has become the most vicious animal of all!

8   Satan represents all of the so-called sins, as they all lead to physical, mental, or emotional gratification!

9   Satan has been the best friend the church has ever had, as he has kept it in business all these years!

(FIRE)

THE BOOK OF SATAN

THE INFERNAL DIATRIBE

The first book of the Satanic Bible is not an attempt to blaspheme as much as it is a statement of what might be termed "diabolical indignation." The Devil has been attacked by the men of God relentlessly and without reservation. Never has there been an opportunity, short of fiction, for the Dark Prince to speak out in the same manner as the spokesmen of the Lord of the Righteous. The pulpit-pounders of the past have been free to define "good" and "evil" as they see fit, and have gladly smashed into oblivion any who disagree with their lies—both verbally and, at times, physically. Their talk of "charity," when applied to His Infernal Majesty, becomes an empty sham—and most unfairly, too, considering the obvious fact that without their Satanic foe their very religions would collapse. How sad, that the allegorical personage most responsible for the success of spiritual religions is shown the *least* amount of charity and the most consistent abuse—and by those who most unctuously preach the rules of fair play! For all the centuries of shouting-down the Devil has received, he has never shouted back at his detractors. He has remained the gentleman at all times, while those he supports rant and rave. He has shown himself to be a model of deportment, but now he feels it is time to shout back. He has decided it is finally time to receive his due. Now the ponderous rule-books of hypocrisy are no longer needed. In order to relearn the Law of the Jungle, a small, slim diatribe will do. Each verse is an inferno. Each word is a tongue of fire. The flames of Hell burn fierce . . . and purify! Read on and learn the Law.

THE
BOOK OF
SATAN

I

1   In this arid wilderness of steel and stone I raise up my voice that you may hear. To the East and to the West I beckon. To the North and to the South I show a sign proclaiming: Death to the weakling, wealth to the strong!

2   Open your eyes that you may see, Oh men of mildewed minds, and listen to me ye bewildered millions!

3   For I stand forth to challenge the wisdom of the world; to interrogate the "laws" of man and of "God"!

4   I request reasons for your golden rule and ask the why and wherefore of your ten commands.

5   Before none of your printed idols do I bend in acquiescence, and he who saith "thou shalt" to me is my mortal foe!

6   I dip my forefinger in the watery blood of your impotent mad redeemer, and write over his thorn-torn brow: The TRUE prince of evil—the king of the slaves!

7   No hoary falsehood shall be a truth to me; no stifling dogma shall encramp my pen!

8   I break away from all conventions that do not lead to my earthly success and happiness.

9   I raise up in stern invasion the standard of the strong!

10   I gaze into the glassy eye of your fearsome Jehovah, and pluck him by the beard; I uplift a broad-axe, and split open his worm-eaten skull!

11   I blast out the ghastly contents of philosophically whited sepulchers and laugh with sardonic wrath!

II

1 Behold the crucifix; what does it symbolize? Pallid incompetence hanging on a tree.

2 I question all things. As I stand before the festering and varnished facades of your haughtiest moral dogmas, I write thereon in letters of blazing scorn: Lo and behold; all this is fraud!

3 Gather around me, Oh! ye death-defiant, and the earth itself shall be thine, to have and to hold!

4 Too long the dead hand has been permitted to sterilize living thought!

5 Too long right and wrong, good and evil have been inverted by false prophets!

6 No creed must be accepted upon authority of a "divine" nature. Religions must be put to the question. No moral dogma must be taken for granted—no standard of measurement deified. There is nothing inherently sacred about moral codes. Like the wooden idols of long ago, they are the work of human hands, and what man has made, man can destroy!

7 He that is slow to believe anything and everything is of great understanding, for belief in one false principle is the beginning of all unwisdom.

8 The chief duty of every new age is to upraise new men to determine its liberties, to lead it towards material success—to rend the rusty padlocks and chains of dead custom that always prevent healthy expansion. Theories and ideas that may have meant life and hope and freedom for our ancestors may now mean destruction, slavery, and dishonor to us!

9 As environments change, no human ideal standeth sure!

10 Whenever, therefore, a lie has built unto itself a throne, let it be assailed without pity and without regret, for under

the domination of an inconvenient falsehood, no one can prosper.

11 Let established sophisms be dethroned, rooted out, burnt and destroyed, for they are a standing menace to all true nobility of thought and action!

12 Whatever alleged "truth" is proven by results to be but an empty fiction, let it be unceremoniously flung into the outer darkness, among the dead gods, dead empires, dead philosophies, and other useless lumber and wreckage!

13 The most dangerous of all enthroned lies is the holy, the sanctified, the privileged lie—the lie everyone believes to be a model truth. It is the fruitful mother of all other popular errors and delusions. It is a hydra-headed tree of unreason with a thousand roots. It is a social cancer!

14 The lie that is known to be a lie is half eradicated, but the lie that even intelligent persons accept as fact—the lie that has been inculcated in a little child at its mother's knee—is more dangerous to contend against than a creeping pestilence!

15 Popular lies have ever been the most potent enemies of personal liberty. There is only one way to deal with them: Cut them out, to the very core, just as cancers. Exterminate them root and branch. Annihilate them, or they will us!

III

1 "Love one another" it has been said is the supreme law, but what power made it so? Upon what rational authority does the gospel of love rest? Why should I not hate mine enemies—if I "love" them does that not place me at their mercy?

2 Is it natural for enemies to do good unto each other—and WHAT IS GOOD?

3 Can the torn and bloody victim "love" the blood-splashed jaws that rend him limb from limb?

4   Are we not all predatory animals by instinct? If humans ceased wholly from preying upon each other, could they continue to exist?

5   Is not "lust and carnal desire" a more truthful term to describe "love" when applied to the continuance of the race? Is not the "love" of the fawning scriptures simply a euphemism for sexual activity, or was the "great teacher" a glorifier of eunuchs?

6   Love your enemies and do good to them that hate and use you—is this not the despicable philosophy of the spaniel that rolls upon its back when kicked?

7   Hate your enemies with a whole heart, and if a man smite you on one cheek, SMASH him on the other!; smite him hip and thigh, for self-preservation is the highest law!

8   He who turns the other cheek is a cowardly dog!

9   Give blow for blow, scorn for scorn, doom for doom— with compound interest liberally added thereunto! Eye for eye, tooth for tooth, aye four-fold, a hundred-fold! Make yourself a Terror to your adversary, and when he goeth his way, he will possess much additional wisdom to ruminate over. Thus shall you make yourself respected in all the walks of life, and your spirit—your *immortal* spirit—shall live, not in an intangible paradise, but in the brains and sinews of those whose respect you have gained.

IV

1   Life is the great indulgence—death, the great abstinence. Therefore, make the most of life—HERE AND NOW!

2   There is no heaven of glory bright, and no hell where sinners roast. Here and now is our day of torment! Here and now is our day of joy! Here and now is our opportunity! Choose ye this day, this hour, for no redeemer liveth!

3   Say unto thine own heart, "I am mine own redeemer."

4   Stop the way of them that would persecute you. Let those

who devise thine undoing be hurled back to confusion and infamy. Let them be as chaff before the cyclone and after they have fallen rejoice in thine own salvation.

5 Then all thy bones shall say pridefully, "Who is like unto me? Have I not been too strong for mine adversaries? Have I not delivered MYSELF by mine own brain and body?"

V

1 Blessed are the strong, for they shall possess the earth—Cursed are the weak, for they shall inherit the yoke!

2 Blessed are the powerful, for they shall be reverenced among men—Cursed are the feeble, for they shall be blotted out!

3 Blessed are the bold, for they shall be masters of the world—Cursed are the righteously humble, for they shall be trodden under cloven hoofs!

4 Blessed are the victorious, for victory is the basis of right—Cursed are the vanquished, for they shall be vassals forever!

5 Blessed are the iron-handed, for the unfit shall flee before them—Cursed are the poor in spirit, for they shall be spat upon!

6 Blessed are the death-defiant, for their days shall be long in the land—Cursed are the gazers toward a richer life beyond the grave, for they shall perish amidst plenty!

7 Blessed are the destroyers of false hope, for they are the true Messiahs—Cursed are the god-adorers, for they shall be shorn sheep!

8 Blessed are the valiant, for they shall obtain great treasure—Cursed are the believers in good and evil, for they are frightened by shadows!

9 Blessed are those that believe in what is best for them, for never shall their minds be terrorized—Cursed are the "lambs of God," for they shall be bled whiter than snow!

10 Blessed is the man who has a sprinkling of enemies, for they shall make him a hero—Cursed is he who doeth good unto others who sneer upon him in return, for he shall be despised!

11 Blessed are the mighty-minded, for they shall ride the whirlwinds—Cursed are they who teach lies for truth and truth for lies, for they are an abomination!

12 Thrice cursed are the weak whose insecurity makes them vile, for they shall serve and suffer!

13 The angel of self-deceit is camped in the souls of the "righteous"—The eternal flame of power through joy dwelleth within the flesh of the Satanist!

THE BOOK OF LUCIFER

THE ENLIGHTENMENT

The Roman god, Lucifer, was the bearer of light, the spirit of the air, the personification of enlightenment. In Christian mythology he became synonymous with evil, which was only to have been expected from a religion whose very existence is perpetuated by clouded definitions and bogus values! It is time to set the record straight. False moralisms and occult inaccuracies must be corrected. Entertaining as they might be, most stories and plays about Devil worship must be recognized as the obsolete absurdities they are. It has been said "the truth will make men free." The truth alone has never set anyone free. It is only DOUBT which will bring mental emancipation. Without the wonderful element of doubt, the doorway through which truth passes would be tightly shut, impervious to the most strenuous poundings of a thousand Lucifers. How understandable that Holy Scripture should refer to the Infernal monarch as the "father of lies"—a magnificent example of character inversion. If one is to believe this theological accusation that the Devil represents falsehood, then it surely must be concurred that it was HE, NOT GOD, THAT ESTABLISHED ALL SPIRITUAL RELIGIONS AND WHO WROTE ALL OF THE HOLY BIBLES! When one doubt is followed by another, the bubble, grown large from long accumulated fallacies, threatens to burst. For those who already doubt supposed truths, this book is revelation. Then Lucifer will have risen. Now is the time for doubt! The bubble of falsehood is bursting and its sound is the roar of the world!

—WANTED!—
GOD
DEAD OR ALIVE

IT is a popular misconception that the Satanist does not believe in God. The concept of "God," as interpreted by man, has been so varied throughout the ages, that the Satanist simply accepts the definition which suits him best. Man has always created his gods, rather than his gods creating *him*. God is, to some, benign—to others, terrifying. To the Satanist "God"—by whatever name he is called, or by no name at all—is seen as the balancing factor in nature, and not as being concerned with suffering. This powerful force which permeates and balances the universe is far too impersonal to care about the happiness or misery of flesh-and-blood creatures on this ball of dirt upon which we live.

Anyone who thinks of *Satan* as evil should consider all the men, women, children, and animals who have died because it was "God's will." Certainly a person grieving the untimely loss of a loved one would much rather have their loved one with them than in God's hands! Instead, they are unctuously consoled by their clergyman who says, "It was God's will, my dear"; or "He is in God's hands now, my son." Such phrases have been a convenient way for religionists to condone or excuse the mercilessness of God. But if God is in complete control and as benign as he is supposed to be, why does He allow these things to happen? Too long have religionists been falling back on their bibles and rulebooks to prove or disprove, justify, condemn, or interpret.

The Satanist realizes that man, and the action and reaction of the universe, is responsible for everything, and doesn't mislead himself into thinking that someone cares. No longer will we sit back and accept "fate" without doing anything about it, just because it says so in Chapter such and such, Psalm so and so—and that's that! The Satanist knows that praying does absolutely no good—in fact, it actually lessens the chance of success, for the devoutly religious too often sit back complacently and pray for a situation which, if they were to do something about it on their own, could be accomplished much quicker!

The Satanist shuns terms such as "hope" and "prayer" as they are indicative of apprehension. If we hope and pray for something to come about, we will not act in a positive way which will *make* it happen. The Satanist, realizing that anything he gets is of his own doing, takes command of the situation instead of praying to God for it to happen. Positive thinking and positive *action* add up to results.

Just as the Satanist does not pray to God for assistance, he does not pray for forgiveness for his wrong doings. In other religions, when one commits a wrong he either prays to God for forgiveness, or confesses to an intermediary and asks *him* to pray to God for forgiveness for his sins. The Satanist knows that if praying does no good, confessing to another human being, like himself, accomplishes even less—and is, furthermore, degrading.

When a Satanist commits a wrong, he realizes that it is natural to make a mistake—and if he is truly sorry about what he has done, he will learn from it and take care not to do the same thing again. If he is not honestly sorry about what he has done, and knows he will do the same thing over and over, he has no business confessing and asking forgiveness in the first place. But this is exactly what happens. People confess their sins

41

so that they can clear their consciences—and be free to go out and sin again, usually the same sin.

There are as many different interpretations of God, in the usual sense of the word, as there are types of people. The images run from a belief in a god who is some vague sort of "universal cosmic mind" to an anthropomorphic deity with a long white beard and sandals who keeps track of every action of each individual.

Even within the confines of a given religion, the personal interpretations of God differ greatly. Some religions actually go so far as to label anyone who belongs to a religious sect other than their own a heretic, even though the overall doctrines and impressions of godliness are nearly the same. For example: The Catholics believe that the Protestants are doomed to Hell simply because they do not belong to the Catholic Church. In the same way, many splinter groups of the Christian faith, such as the evangelical or revivalist churches, believe that the Catholics are heathens who worship graven images. (Christ is depicted in the image that is most physiologically akin to the individual worshipping him, and yet the Christians criticize "heathens" for the worship of graven images.) And the Jews have always been given the Devil's name.

Even though the god in all of these religions is basically the same, each regards the way chosen by the others as reprehensible, and to top it all, religionists actually PRAY for one another! They have scorn for their brothers of the right-hand path because their religions carry different labels, and somehow this animosity must be released. What better way than through "prayer"! What a simperingly polite way of saying: "I hate your guts," is the thinly disguised device known as praying for your enemy! Praying for one's own enemy is nothing more than bargain-basement anger, and of a decidedly shoddy and inferior quality!

If there has been so much violent discrepancy as to the proper way in which to worship God, how many different interpretations of God can there be—and *who* is right?

All devout "white-lighters" are concerned with pleasing

God so that they might have the "Pearly Gates" opened for them when they die. Nevertheless, if a man has *not* lived his life in accordance with the regulations of his faith, he *can* at the last minute call a clergyman to his deathbed for final absolution. The priest or minister will then come running, on the double, to "make everything right" with God and see to it that his passport to the Heavenly Realm is in order. (The Yezidis, a sect of Devil worshippers, take a different viewpoint. They believe that God is all-powerful, but also all-forgiving, and so accordingly feel that it is the *Devil* whom they must please, as he is the one who rules their lives while here on earth. They believe so strongly that God will forgive all of their sins once they have been given the last rites, that they feel no need to concern themselves with the opinion God may hold of them while they live.)

With all of the contradictions in the Christian scriptures, many people currently cannot rationally accept Christianity the way it has been practiced in the past. Great numbers of people are beginning to doubt the existence of God, in the established Christian sense of the word. So, they have taken to calling themselves "Christian Atheists." True, the Christian Bible is a mass of contradictions; but what could be more contradictory than the term "Christian Atheist"?

If prominent *leaders* of the Christian faith are rejecting the past interpretation of God, how then can their *followers* be expected to adhere to previous religious tradition?

With all the debates about whether or not God is dead, if he isn't he had better have MEDICARE!

THE GOD YOU SAVE
MAY BE YOURSELF

ALL religions of a spiritual nature are inventions of man. He has created an entire system of gods with nothing more than his carnal brain. Just because he has an ego and cannot accept it, he has had to externalize it into some great spiritual device which he calls "God."

God can do all the things man is forbidden to do—such as kill people, perform miracles to gratify his will, control without any apparent responsibility, etc. If man needs such a god and recognizes that god, then he is worshipping an entity that a human being invented. Therefore, HE IS WORSHIPPING BY PROXY THE MAN THAT INVENTED GOD. Is it not more sensible to worship a god that he, himself, has created, in accordance with his own emotional needs—one that best represents the very carnal and physical being that has the idea-power to invent a god *in the first place*?

If man insists on externalizing his true self in the form of "God," then why fear his true self, in fearing "God,"—why praise his true self in praising "God,"—why remain externalized from "God" IN ORDER TO ENGAGE IN RITUAL AND RELIGIOUS CEREMONY IN HIS NAME?

Man needs ritual and dogma, but no law states that an *externalized* god is necessary in order to engage in ritual and ceremony performed in a god's name! Could it be that when he closes the gap between himself and his "God" he sees the demon of pride creeping forth—that very embodiment of

44

Lucifer appearing in his midst? He no longer can view himself in two parts, the carnal and the spiritual, but sees them merge as one, and then to his abysmal horror, discovers that they are only the carnal—AND ALWAYS WERE! Then he either hates himself to death, day by day—or rejoices that he is what he is!

If he hates himself, he searches out new and more complex spiritual paths of "enlightenment" in hopes that he may split himself up again in his quest for stronger and more externalized "gods" to scourge his poor miserable shell. If he accepts himself, but recognizes that ritual and ceremony are the important devices that his invented religions have utilized to sustain his faith *in a lie*, then it is the SAME FORM OF RITUAL that will sustain his faith *in the truth*—the primitive pageantry that will give his awareness of his own majestic being added substance.

When all religious faith in lies has waned, it is because man has become closer to himself and farther from "God"; closer to the "Devil." If this is what the devil represents, and a man lives his life in the devil's fane, with the sinews of Satan moving his flesh, then he either escapes from the cacklings and carpings of the righteous, or stands proudly in his secret places of the earth and manipulates the folly-ridden masses through his own Satanic might, until that day when he may come forth in splendor proclaiming "I AM A SATANIST! BOW DOWN, FOR I AM THE HIGHEST EMBODIMENT OF HUMAN LIFE!"

SOME EVIDENCE OF
A NEW SATANIC AGE

THE seven deadly sins of the Christian Church are: greed, pride, envy, anger, gluttony, lust, and sloth. Satanism advocates indulging in each of these "sins" as they all lead to physical, mental, or emotional gratification.

A Satanist knows there is nothing wrong with being greedy, as it only means that he wants more than he already has. Envy means to look with favor upon the possessions of others, and to be desirous of obtaining similar things for oneself. Envy and greed are the motivating forces of ambition—and without ambition, very little of any importance would be accomplished.

Gluttony is simply eating more than you need to keep yourself alive. When you have overeaten to the point of obesity, another sin—pride—will motivate you to regain an appearance that will renew your self-respect.

Anyone who buys an article of clothing for a purpose other than covering his body and protecting it from the elements is guilty of pride. Satanists often encounter scoffers who maintain that labels are not necessary. It must be pointed out to these destroyers of labels that one or many articles they themselves are wearing are not necessary to keep them warm. There is not a person on this earth who is completely devoid of ornamentation. The Satanist points out that any ornamentation of the scoffer's body shows that he, too, is guilty of pride. Regardless of how verbose the cynic may be in his intellectual description of how free he is, he is still wearing the elements of pride.

Being reluctant to get up in the morning is to be guilty of sloth, and if you lie in bed long enough you may find yourself committing yet another sin—lust. To have the faintest stirring of sexual desire is to be guilty of lust. In order to insure the propagation of humanity, nature made lust the second most powerful instinct, the first being self-preservation. Realizing this, the Christian Church made fornication the "Original Sin." In this way they made sure no one would escape sin. Your very state of being is as a result of sin—the *Original* sin!

The strongest instinct in every living thing is self-preservation, which brings us to the last of the seven deadly sins—anger. Is it not our instinct for self-preservation that is aroused when someone harms us, when we become angry enough to protect ourselves from further attack? A Satanist practices the motto, "If a man smite thee on one cheek, *smash* him on the other!" Let no wrong go unredressed. Be as a lion in the path—be dangerous even in defeat!

Since man's natural instincts lead him to sin, all men are sinners; and all sinners go to hell. If everyone goes to hell, then you will meet all your friends there. Heaven must be populated with some rather strange creatures if all they lived for was to go to a place where they can strum harps for eternity.

"Times have changed. Religious leaders no longer preach that all our natural actions are sinful. We no longer think sex is dirty—or that taking pride in ourselves is shameful—or that wanting something someone else has is vicious." Of course not, times have changed! "If you want proof of this, just look at how liberal the churches have become. Why, they're practicing all the things that you preach."

Satanists hear these, and similar statements, all the time; and they agree wholeheartedly. BUT, if the world has changed so much, why continue to grasp at the threads of a dying faith? If many religions are denying their own scriptures because they are out of date, and are preaching the philosophies of Satanism, why not call it by its rightful name—Satanism? Certainly it would be far less hypocritical.

In recent years there has been an attempt to humanize the spiritual concept of Christianity. This has manifested itself in the most obvious non-spiritual means. Masses which had been said in Latin are now said in native languages—which only succeeds in making the nonsense easier to understand, and at the same time robs the ceremony of the esoteric nature which is consistent with the tenets of the dogma. It is much simpler to obtain an emotional reaction using words and phrases that cannot be understood than it is with statements which even the simplest mind will question when hearing them in an understandable language.

If priests and ministers were to have used the devices to fill their churches one hundred years ago that they use today, they would have been charged with heresy, called devils, oft-times persecuted, but certainly excommunicated without hesitation.

The religionists wail, "We must keep up with the times," forgetting that, due to the limiting factors and deeply engrained laws of white light religions, there can *never* be sufficient change to meet the needs of man.

Past religions have always represented the spiritual nature of man, with little or no concern for his carnal or mundane needs. They have considered this life but transitory, and the flesh merely a shell; physical pleasure trivial, and pain a worthwhile preparation for the "Kingdom of God." How well the utter hypocrisy comes forth when the "righteous" make a change in their religion to keep up with man's natural change! The only way that Christianity can ever completely serve the needs of man is to become as Satanism is NOW.

It has become necessary for a NEW religion, based on man's natural instincts, to come forth. THEY have named it. It is called Satanism. It is that power condemned that has caused the religious controversy over birth-control measures—a disgruntled admission that sexual activity, for fun, is here to stay.

It is the "Devil" who caused women to show their legs, to

titillate men—the same kind of legs, now socially acceptable to gaze upon, which are revealed by young nuns as they walk about in their shortened habits. What a delightful step in the right (or left) direction! Is it possible we will soon see "topless" nuns sensually throwing their bodies about to the "Missa Solemnis Rock"? Satan smiles and says he would like that fine— many nuns are very pretty girls with nice legs.

Many churches with some of the largest congregations have the most hand-clapping, sensual music—also Satanically inspired. After all, the Devil has always had the best tunes.

Church picnics, despite all of Aunt Martha's talk about the Lord's Bountiful Harvest, are nothing more than a good excuse for Sunday gluttony; and everyone knows that lots more than Bible reading goes on in the bushes.

The fund-raising adjunct to many church bazaars is commonly known as a carnival, which used to mean the celebration of the flesh; now a carnival is okay because the money goes to the church so that it can preach against the temptations of the Devil! It will be said that these things are only pagan devices and ceremonies—that the Christians borrowed them. True, but the Pagans revelled in the delights of the flesh, and were condemned by the very same people who celebrate their rituals, but call them by different names.

Priests and ministers are in the front lines of peace demonstrations, and lying on railroad tracks in front of trains carrying war materials, with as much dedication as their brothers of the cloth, from the same seminaries, who are blessing the bullets and bombs and fighting men as chaplains in the armed forces. Someone must be wrong, someplace. Could it be that Satan is the one qualified to act as accuser? Certainly they named him that!

When a puppy reaches maturity it becomes a dog; when ice melts it is called water; when twelve months have been used up, we get a new calendar with the proper chronological name; when "magic" becomes scientific fact we refer to it as medicine, astronomy, etc. When one name is no longer appropriate for a given thing it is only logical to change it to a new one which better fits the subject. Why, then, do we not follow suit in the area of religion? Why continue to call a religion the same name when the tenets of that religion no longer fit the original one? Or, if the religion *does* preach the same things that it always has, but its followers practice nearly none of its teachings, why do they continue to call themselves by the name given to followers of that religion?

If you do not believe in what your religion teaches, why continue to support a belief which is contradictory with your feelings. You would never vote for a person or issue you did not believe in, so why cast your ecclesiastical vote for a religion which is not consistent with your convictions? You have no right to complain about a political situation you have voted for or supported in any way—which includes sitting back and complacently agreeing with neighbors who approve the situation, just because you are too lazy or cowardly to speak your mind. So it is with religious balloting. Even if you cannot be aggressively honest about your opinions because of unfavorable consequences from employers, community leaders, etc., you can, at least, be honest with yourself. In the privacy of your own home and with close friends you *must* support the religion which has YOUR best interests at heart.

"Satanism is based on a very sound philosophy," say the emancipated. "But why call it Satanism? Why not call it something like 'Humanism' or a name that would have the connotation of a witchcraft group, something a little more esoteric —something less blatant." There is more than one reason for this. Humanism is not a religion. It is simply a way of life with no ceremony or dogma. Satanism has both ceremony and dogma. Dogma, as will be explained, is necessary.

Satanism differs greatly from all other so-called white-light, "white" witchcraft or magical groups in the world today. These self-righteous and supercilious religions protest that *their* members use the powers of magic only for altruistic purposes. Satanists look with disdain upon "white" witchcraft groups because they feel that altruism is sinning on the lay-away plan. It is unnatural not to have the desire to gain things for yourself.

Satanism represents a form of controlled selfishness. This does not mean that you never do anything for anyone else. If you do something to make someone for whom you care happy, his happiness will give you a sense of gratification.

Satanism advocates practicing a modified form of the Golden Rule. Our interpretation of this rule is: "Do unto others as they do unto you"; because if you "Do unto others as you would have them do unto you," and they, in turn, treat you badly, it goes against human nature to continue to treat them with consideration. You should do unto others as you would have them do unto you, but if your courtesy is not returned, they should be treated with the wrath they deserve.

White witchcraft groups say that if you curse a person, it will return to you three-fold, come home to roost, or in some way boomerang back to the sender. This is yet another indication of the guilt-ridden philosophy which is held by these neo-Pagan, pseudo-Christian groups. White witches want to delve into witchcraft, but cannot divorce themselves from the stigma attached to it. Therefore, they call themselves white magicians, and base seventy-five per cent of their philosophy on the trite and hackneyed tenets of Christianity. Anyone who pretends to be interested in magic or the occult for reasons other than gaining personal power is the worst kind of hypocrite. The Satanist respects Christianity for, at least, being consistent in its guilt-ridden philosophy, but can only feel contempt for people who attempt to appear emancipated from guilt by joining a witchcraft group, and then practice the same basic philosophy as Christianity.

White magic is supposedly utilized only for good or unselfish purposes, and black magic, we are told, is used only for selfish or "evil" reasons. Satanism draws no such dividing line. Magic is magic, be it used to help or hinder. The Satanist, being the magician, should have the ability to decide what is just, and then apply the powers of magic to attain his goals.

During white magical ceremonies, the practitioners stand within a pentagram to protect themselves from the "evil" forces which they call upon for help. To the Satanist, it seems a bit two-faced to call on these forces for help, while at the same time protecting yourself from the very powers you have asked for assistance. The Satanist realizes that only by putting himself in league with these forces can he fully and unhypocritically utilize the Powers of Darkness to his best advantage.

In a Satanic magical ceremony, the participants do NOT: join hands and dance "ring around the rosy" in a circle; burn candles of various colors for various wishes; call out the names of "Father, Son, and Holy Ghost" while supposedly practicing the Black Arts; pick a "Saint" for their personal guide in obtaining help for their problems; dunk themselves in smelly oils and hope the money comes in; meditate so they can arrive at a "great spiritual awakening"; recite long incantations with the name of Jesus thrown in for good measure, between every few words, etc., etc., etc., *ad nauseam!*

BECAUSE—This is NOT the way to practice Satanic magic. If you cannot divorce yourself from hypocritical self-deceit you will never be successful as a magician, much less a Satanist.

The Satanic religion has not merely lifted the coin—it has flipped it completely over. Therefore, why should it support the very principles to which it is completely opposed by calling itself anything other than a name which is totally in keeping with the *reversed* doctrines which make up the Satanic philosophy? Satanism is not a white light religion; it is a religion of the flesh, the mundane, the carnal—all of which are ruled by Satan, the personification of the Left Hand Path.

Inevitably, the next question asked is: "Granted, you can't call it humanism because humanism is not a religion; but why even have a religion in the first place if all you do is what comes naturally, anyway? Why not just do it?"

Modern man has come a long way; he has become disenchanted with the nonsensical dogmas of past religions. We are living in an enlightened age. Psychiatry has made great strides in enlightening man about his true personality. We are living in an era of intellectual awareness unlike any the world has ever seen.

This is all very well and good, BUT—there is one flaw in

this new state of awareness. It is one thing to accept something intellectually, but to accept the same thing emotionally is an entirely different matter. The one need that psychiatry cannot fill is man's inherent need for emotionalizing through dogma. Man needs ceremony and ritual, fantasy and enchantment. Psychiatry, despite all the good it has done, has robbed man of wonder and fantasy which religion, in the past, has provided.

Satanism, realizing the current needs of man, fills the large grey void between religion and psychiatry. The Satanic philosophy *combines* the fundamentals of psychology *and* good, honest emotionalizing, or dogma. It provides man with his much needed fantasy. There is nothing wrong with dogma, providing it is not based on ideas and actions which go completely against human nature.

The quickest way of traveling between two points is in a straight line. If all the guilts that have been built up can be turned into advantages, it eliminates the need for intellectual purging of the psyche in an attempt to cleanse it from these repressions. Satanism is the only religion known to man that accepts man as he is, and promotes the rationale of turning a bad thing into a good thing rather than bending over backwards to eliminate the bad thing.

Therefore, after intellectually evaluating your problems through common sense and drawing on what psychiatry has taught us, if you *still* cannot emotionally release yourself from unwarranted guilt, and put your theories into action, then you should learn to make your guilt work *for* you. You should act upon your natural instincts, and then, if you cannot perform without feeling guilty, revel in your guilt. This may sound like a contradiction in terms, but if you will think about it, guilt can often add a fillip to the senses. Adults would do well to take a lesson from children. Children often take great delight in doing something they know they are not supposed to.

Yes, times have changed, but man hasn't. The basics of Satanism have always existed. The only thing that *is* new is the formal organization of a religion based on the universal traits of man. For centuries, magnificent structures of stone, concrete, mortar, and steel have been devoted to man's abstinence. It is high time that human beings stopped fighting themselves, and devoted their time to building temples designed for man's indulgences.

Even though times have changed, and always will, man remains basically the same. For two thousand years man has done penance for something he never should have had to feel guilty about in the first place. We are tired of denying ourselves the pleasures of life which we deserve. Today, as always, man needs to enjoy himself here and now, instead of waiting for his rewards in heaven. So, why not have a religion based on indulgence? Certainly it is consistent with the nature of the beast. We are no longer supplicating weaklings trembling before an unmerciful "God" who cares not whether we live or die. We are self-respecting, prideful people—we are Satanists!

HELL, THE DEVIL,
AND HOW TO
SELL YOUR SOUL

SATAN has certainly been the best friend the church has ever had, as he has kept it in business all these years. The false doctrine of Hell and the Devil has allowed the Protestant and Catholic Churches to flourish far too long. Without a devil to point their fingers at, religionists of the right hand path would have nothing with which to threaten their followers. "Satan leads you to temptation"; "Satan is the prince of evil"; "Satan is vicious, cruel, brutal," they warn. "If you give in to the temptations of the devil, you will surely suffer eternal damnation and roast in Hell."

The semantic meaning of Satan is the "adversary" or "opposition" or the "accuser." The very word "devil" comes from the Indian *devi* which means "god." Satan represents opposition to all religions which serve to frustrate and condemn man for his natural instincts. He has been given an evil role simply because he represents the carnal, earthly, and mundane aspects of life.

Satan, the chief devil of the Western World, was originally an angel whose duty it was to report human delinquencies to God. It was not until the Fourteenth Century that he began to be depicted as an evil deity who was part man and part animal, with goat-like horns and hooves. Before Christianity gave him the names of Satan, Lucifer, etc., the carnal side of man's nature was governed by the god which was then called Dionysus, or Pan, depicted as a satyr or faun, by the Greeks. Pan was originally the "good guy," and symbolized fertility and fecundity.

Whenever a nation comes under a new form of government, the heroes of the past become the villains of the present. So it is with religion. The earliest Christians believed that the Pagan deities were devils, and to employ them was to use "black magic." Miraculous heavenly events they termed "white magic"; this was the sole distinction between the two. The old gods did not die, they fell into Hell and became devils. The bogey, goblin, or bugaboo used to frighten children is derived from the Slavonic "Bog" which means "god," as does Bhaga in Hindu.

Many pleasures revered before the advent of Christianity were condemned by the new religion. It required little change-over to transform the horns and cloven hooves of Pan into a most convincing devil! Pan's attributes could be neatly changed into charged-with-punishment sins, and so the metamorphosis was complete.

The association of the goat with the Devil is found in the Christian Bible, where the holiest day of the year, the Day of Atonement, was celebrated by casting lots for two goats "without blemish," one to be offered to the Lord, and one to Azazel. The goat carrying the sins of the people was driven into the desert and became a "scapegoat." This is the origin of the goat which is still used in lodge ceremonies today as it was also used in Egypt, where once a year it was sacrificed to a God.

The devils of mankind are many, and their origins diversified. The performance of Satanic ritual does *not* embrace the calling forth of demons; this practice is followed only by those who are in fear of the very forces they conjure.

Supposedly, demons are malevolent spirits with attributes conducive to the deterioration of the people or events that they touch upon. The Greek word *demon* meant a guardian spirit or source of inspiration, and to be sure, later theologians invented legion upon legion of these harbingers of inspiration—all wicked.

An indication of the cowardice of "magicians" of the right-hand path is the practice of calling upon a particular demon (who would supposedly be a minion of the devil) to do his bidding. The assumption is that the demon, being only a flunky of the devil, is easier to control. Occult lore states that only the most formidably "protected" or insanely foolhardy sorcerer would try to call forth the Devil himself.

The Satanist does not furtively call upon these "lesser" devils, but brazenly invokes those who people that infernal army of long-standing outrage—*the Devils themselves!*

Theologians have catalogued some of the names of devils in their lists of demons, as might be expected, but the roster which follows contains the names most effectively used in Satanic ritual. These are the names and origins of the Gods and Goddesses called upon, which make up a large part of the occupancy of the Royal Palace of Hell:

THE FOUR CROWN PRINCES OF HELL

SATAN—*(Hebrew)* adversary, opposite, accuser, Lord of fire, the inferno, the south

LUCIFER—*(Roman)* bringer of light, enlightenment, the air, the morning star, the east

BELIAL—*(Hebrew)* without a master, baseness of the earth, independence, the north

LEVIATHAN—*(Hebrew)* the serpent out of the deeps, the sea, the west

THE INFERNAL NAMES

Abaddon—*(Hebrew)* the destroyer

Adramelech—Samarian devil

Ahpuch—Mayan devil

Ahriman—Mazdean devil

Amon—Egyptian ram-headed god of life and reproduction

Apollyon—Greek synonym for Satan, the arch fiend

Asmodeus—Hebrew devil of sensuality and luxury, originally "creature of judgement"

Astaroth—Phoenician goddess of lasciviousness, equivalent of Babylonian Ishtar

Azazel—*(Hebrew)* taught man to make weapons of war, introduced cosmetics

Baalberith—Canaanite Lord of the covenant who was later made a devil

Balaam—Hebrew devil of avarice and greed

Baphomet—worshipped by the Templars as symbolic of Satan

Bast—Egyptian goddess of pleasure represented by the cat

Beelzebub—*(Hebrew)* Lord of the Flies, taken from symbolism of the scarab

Behemoth—Hebrew personification of Satan in the form of an elephant

Beherit—Syriac name for Satan

Bilé—Celtic god of Hell

Chemosh—national god of Moabites, later a devil

Cimeries—rides a black horse and rules Africa

Coyote—American Indian devil

Dagon—Philistine avenging devil of the sea

Damballa—Voodoo serpent god

Demogorgon—Greek name of the devil, it is said should not be known to mortals

Diabolus—*(Greek)* "flowing downwards"

Dracula—Romanian name for devil

Emma-O—Japanese ruler of Hell

Euronymous—Greek prince of death

Fenriz—son of Loki, depicted as a wolf

Gorgo—dim. of Demogorgon, Greek name of the devil

Haborym—Hebrew synonym for Satan

Hecate—Greek goddess of the underworld and witchcraft

Ishtar—Babylonian goddess of fertility

Kali—*(Hindu)* daughter of Shiva, high priestess of the Thuggees

Lilith—Hebrew female devil, Adam's first wife who taught him the ropes

Loki—Teutonic devil

Mammon—Aramaic god of wealth and profit

Mania—Etruscan goddess of Hell

Mantus—Etruscan god of Hell

Marduk—god of the city of Babylon

Mastema—Hebrew synonym for Satan

Melek Taus—Yezidi devil

Mephistopheles—*(Greek)* he who shuns the light, q. v. Faust

Metztli—Aztec goddess of the night

Mictian—Aztec god of death

Midgard—son of Loki, depicted as a serpent

Milcom—Ammonite devil

Moloch—Phoenician and Canaanite devil

Mormo—*(Greek)* King of the Ghouls, consort of Hecate

Naamah—Hebrew female devil of seduction

Nergal—Babylonian god of Hades

Nihasa—American Indian devil

Nija—Polish god of the underworld

O-Yama—Japanese name for Satan

Pan—Greek god of lust, later relegated to devildom

Pluto—Greek god of the underworld

Proserpine—Greek queen of the underworld

Pwcca—Welsh name for Satan

Rimmon—Syrian devil worshipped at Damascus

Sabazios—Phrygian origin, identified with Dionysos, snake worship

Saitan—Enochian equivalent of Satan

Sammael—*(Hebrew)* "venom of God"

Samnu—Central Asian devil

Sedit—American Indian devil

Sekhmet—Egyptian goddess of vengeance

Set—Egyptian devil

Shaitan—Arabic name for Satan

Shiva—*(Hindu)* the destroyer

Supay—Inca god of the underworld

T'an-mo—Chinese counterpart to the devil, covetousness, desire

Tchort—Russian name for Satan, "black god"

Tezcatlipoca—Aztec god of Hell

Thamuz—Sumerian god who later was relegated to devil-dom

Thoth—Egyptian god of magic

Tunrida—Scandinavian female devil

Typhon—Greek personification of Satan

Yaotzin—Aztec god of Hell

Yen-lo-Wang—Chinese ruler of Hell

The devils of past religions have always, at least in part, had animal characteristics, evidence of man's constant need to deny that he too is an animal, for to do so would serve a mighty blow to his impoverished ego.

The pig was despised by the Jews and the Egyptians. It symbolized the gods Frey, Osiris, Adonis, Persephone, Attis, and Demeter, and was sacrificed to Osiris and the Moon. But, in time, it became degraded into a devil. The Phoenicians worshipped a fly god, Baal, from which comes the devil, Beelzebub. Both Baal and Beelzebub are identical to the dung beetle or scarabaeus of the Egyptians which appeared to resurrect itself, much as the mythical bird, the phoenix, rose from its own ashes. The ancient Jews believed, through their contact with the Persians, that the two great forces in the world were Ahura-Mazda, the god of fire, light, life, and goodness; and Ahriman, the serpent, the god of darkness, destruction, death, and evil. These, and countless other examples, not only depict man's devils as animals, but also show his need to sacrifice the original animal gods and demote them to his devils.

At the time of the Reformation, in the Sixteenth Century, the alchemist, Dr. Johann Faustus, discovered a method of summoning a demon—Mephistopheles—from Hell and making a pact with him. He signed a contract in blood to turn his soul over to Mephistopheles in return for the feeling of youth, and at once became young. When the time came for Faustus to die, he retired to his room and was blown to bits as though his laboratory had exploded. This story is a protest of the times (the Sixteenth Century) against science, chemistry, and magic.

To become a Satanist, it is unnecessary to sell your soul to the Devil or make a pact with Satan. This threat was devised by Christianity to terrorize people so they would not stray from the fold. With scolding fingers and trembling voices, they taught their followers that if they gave in to the temptations of Satan, and lived their lives according to their natural predilections, they would have to pay for their sinful pleasures by giving their souls to Satan and suffering in Hell for all eternity. People were led to believe that a pure soul was a passport to everlasting life.

Pious prophets have taught man to fear Satan. But what of terms like "God fearing"? If God is so merciful, why do people have to fear him? Are we to believe there is nowhere we can turn to escape fear? If you have to fear God, why not be "Satan fearing" and at least have the fun that being God fearing denies you? Without such wholesale fear religionists would have had nothing with which to wield power over their followers.

The Teutonic Goddess of the Dead and daughter of Loki was named *Hel*, a Pagan god of torture and punishment. Another "L" was added when the books of the Old Testament were formulated. The prophets who wrote the Bible did not know the word "Hell"; they used the Hebrew *Sheol* and the

61

Greek *Hades*, which meant the grave; also the Greek *Tartaros*, which was the abode of fallen angels, the underworld (inside the earth), and *Gehenna*, which was a valley near Jerusalem where Moloch reigned and garbage was dumped and burned. It is from this that the Christian Church has evolved the idea of "fire and brimstone" in Hell.

The Protestant Hell and the Catholic Hell are places of eternal punishment; however, the Catholics also believe there is a "Purgatory" where all souls go for a time, and a "Limbo" where unbaptized souls go. The Buddhist Hell is divided into eight sections, the first seven of which can be expiated. The ecclesiastical description of Hell is that of a horrible place of fire and torment; in Dante's *Inferno*, and in northern climes, it was thought to be an icy cold region, a giant refrigerator.

(Even with all their threats of eternal damnation and soul roasting, Christian missionaries have run across some who were not so quick to swallow their drivel. Pleasure and pain, like beauty, are in the eye of the beholder. So, when missionaries ventured to Alaska and warned the Eskimos of the horrors of Hell and the blazing lake of fire awaiting transgressors, they eagerly asked: "How do we get there?"!)

Most Satanists do not accept Satan as an anthropomorphic being with cloven hooves, a barbed tail, and horns. He merely represents a force of nature—the powers of darkness which have been named just that because no religion has taken these forces *out* of the darkness. Nor has science been able to apply technical terminology to this force. It is an untapped reservoir that few can make use of because they lack the ability to use a tool without having to first break down and label all the parts which make it run. It is this incessant need to analyze which prohibits most people from taking advantage of this many faceted key to the unknown—which the Satanist chooses to call "Satan."

Satan, as a god, demi-god, personal saviour, or whatever you wish to call him, was invented by the formulators of every religion on the face of the earth for only one purpose—to preside over man's so-called wicked activities and situations here on earth. Consequently, anything resulting in physical or mental gratification was defined as "evil"—thus assuring a lifetime of unwarranted guilt for everyone!

So, if "evil" they have named us, evil we are—and so what! The Satanic Age is upon us! Why not take advantage of it and LIVE! *

---

* (evil reversed)

LOVE AND HATE

SATANISM represents kindness to those who deserve it instead of love wasted on ingrates!

You cannot love everyone; it is ridiculous to think you can. If you love everyone and everything you lose your natural powers of selection and wind up being a pretty poor judge of character and quality. If anything is used too freely it loses its true meaning. Therefore, the Satanist believes you should love strongly and completely those who deserve your love, but never turn the other cheek to your enemy!

Love is one of the most intense emotions felt by man; another is hate. Forcing yourself to feel indiscriminate love is very unnatural. If you try to love everyone you only lessen your feelings for those who deserve your love. Repressed hatred can lead to many physical and emotional ailments. By learning to release your hatred towards those who deserve it, you cleanse yourself of these malignant emotions and need not take your pent-up hatred out on your loved ones.

There has never been a great "love" movement in the history of the world that hasn't wound up killing countless numbers of people, we must assume, to prove how much they loved them! Every hypocrite who ever walked the earth has had pockets bulging with love!

Every pharisaical religionist claims to love his enemies, even though when wronged he consoles himself by thinking "God will punish them." Instead of admitting to themselves that they are capable of hating their foes and treating them in the manner they deserve, they say: "There, but for the grace of God, go I," and "pray" for them. Why should we humiliate and lower ourselves by drawing such inaccurate comparisons?

Satanism has been thought of as being synonymous with cruelty and brutality. This is so only because people are afraid to face the truth—and the truth is that human beings are not all benign or all loving. Just because the Satanist admits he is capable of both love *and* hate, he is considered hateful. On the contrary, because he is able to give vent to his hatred through ritualized expression, he is far *more* capable of love—the deepest kind of love. By honestly recognizing and admitting to both the hate and the love he feels, there is no confusing one emotion with the other. Without being able to experience one of these emotions, you cannot *fully* experience the other.

SATANIC SEX

MUCH controversy has arisen over the Satanic views on "free love." It is often assumed that sexual activity is the most important factor of the Satanic religion, and that willingness to participate in sex-orgies is a prerequisite for becoming a Satanist. Nothing could be farther from the truth! In fact, opportunists who have no deeper interest in Satanism than merely the sexual aspects are emphatically discouraged.

Satanism *does* advocate sexual freedom, but only in the true sense of the word. Free love, in the Satanic concept, means *exactly* that—freedom to either be faithful to one person or to indulge your sexual desires with as many others as you feel is necessary to satisfy your particular needs.

Satanism does *not* encourage orgiastic activity or extramarital affairs for those to whom they do not come naturally. For many, it would be very unnatural and detrimental to be unfaithful to their chosen mates. To others, it would be frustrating to be bound sexually to just one person. Each person must decide for himself what form of sexual activity best suits his individual needs. Self-deceitfully forcing yourself to be adulterous or to have sex partners when not married just for the sake of proving to others (or worse yet, to yourself) that you are emancipated from sexual guilt is just as wrong, by Satanic standards, as leaving any sexual need unfulfilled because of ingrained feelings of guilt.

Many of those who are constantly preoccupied with demonstrating their emancipation from sexual guilt are, in reality, held in *even greater* sexual bondage than those who simply accept sexual activity as a natural part of life and don't make a big to-do over their sexual freedom. For example, it is an established fact that the nymphomaniac (every man's dream girl and heroine of all lurid novels) is not sexually free, but is actually frigid and roves from man to man because she is too inhibited to *ever* find complete sexual release.

Another misconception is the idea that ability to engage in group sexual activity is indicative of sexual freedom. All contemporary free-sex groups have one thing in common—discouragement of fetishistic or deviant activity.

Actually, the most forced examples of non-fetishistic sexual activity thinly disguised as "freedom" have a common format. Each of the participants in an orgy removes all clothing, following the example set forth by one, and mechanically fornicate—also following the leader's example. None of the performers consider that their "emancipated" form of sex might be regarded as regimented and infantile by non-members who fail to equate uniformity with freedom.

The Satanist realizes that if he is to be a sexual connoisseur (and truly free from sexual guilt) he cannot be stifled by the so-called sexual revolutionists any more than he can by the prudery of his guilt-ridden society. These free-sex clubs miss the whole point of sexual freedom. Unless sexual activity can be expressed on an individual basis (which includes personal fetishes), there is absolutely no purpose in belonging to a sexual freedom organization.

Satanism condones any type of sexual activity which properly satisfies your individual desires—be it heterosexual, homosexual, bisexual, or even asexual, if you choose. Satanism also sanctions any fetish or deviation which will enhance your sex-life, so long as it involves no one who does not wish to be involved.

The prevalence of deviant and/or fetishistic behavior in our society would stagger the imagination of the sexually naïve. There are more sexual variants than the unenlightened individual can perceive: transvestism, sadism, masochism, urolagnia, exhibitionism—to name only a few of the more predominant. Everyone has some form of fetish, but because they are unaware of the preponderance of fetishistic activity in our society, they feel they are depraved if they submit to their "unnatural" yearnings.*

Even the asexual has a deviation—his *asexuality*. It is far more abnormal to have a lack of sexual desire (unless illness or old-age, or another *valid* reason has caused the wane) than it is to be sexually promiscuous. However, if a Satanist chooses sexual sublimation above overt sexual expression, that is entirely his own affair. In many cases of sexual sublimation (or asexuality), any attempt to emancipate himself sexually would prove devastating to the asexual.

Asexuals are invariably sexually sublimated by their jobs or hobbies. All the energy and driving interest which would normally be devoted to sexual activity is channelled into other pastimes or into their chosen occupations. If a person favors other interests over sexual activity, it is his right, and no one is justified in condemning him for it. However, the person should at least recognize the fact that this *is* a sexual sublimation.

Because of lack of opportunity for expression, many secret sexual desires never progress beyond the fantasy stage. Lack of release often leads to compulsion and, therefore, a great number of people devise undetectable methods of giving vent to their urges. Just because most fetishistic activity is not outwardly apparent, the sexually unsophisticated should not delude himself into thinking it does not exist. To cite examples of the ingenious techniques used: The male transvestite will indulge in his fetish by wearing feminine undergarments while going

---

* Fetishism is not only practiced by human beings, but by animals, as well. The fetish is an integral ingredient in the sex-lives of animals. The sexual odor, for example, is necessary for one animal to become sexually aroused by another. Laboratory tests have shown that when an animal is scientifically deodorized, it loses sexual attractiveness to the other animals. The stimulation provided by sexual odor is also enjoyed by man, although he will often deny it.

about his daily activities; or the masochistic woman might wear a rubber girdle several sizes too small, so she may derive sexual pleasure from her fetishistic discomfort throughout the day, with no one the wiser. These illustrations are far tamer and more prevalent examples than others which could have been given.

Satanism encourages any form of sexual expression you may desire, *so long as it hurts no one else*. This statement must be qualified, to avoid misinterpretation. By not hurting another, this does not include the unintentional hurt felt by those who might not agree with your views on sex, because of *their* anxieties regarding sexual morality. Naturally, you should avoid offending others who mean a great deal to you, such as prudish friends and relatives. However, if you earnestly endeavor to escape hurting them, and despite your efforts they accidentally find out, you cannot be held responsible, and therefore should feel no guilt as a result of either your sexual convictions, or their being hurt because of those convictions. If you are in constant fear of offending the prudish by your attitude towards sex, then there is no sense in trying to emancipate yourself from sexual guilt. However, no purpose is served by flaunting your permissiveness.

The other exception to the rule regards dealings with masochists. A masochist derives pleasure from *being* hurt; so *denying* the masochist his pleasure-through-pain hurts *him* just as much as actual physical pain hurts the non-masochist. The story of the truly cruel sadist illustrates this point: The masochist says to the sadist, "beat me." To which the merciless sadist replies, "NO!" If a person wants to be hurt and enjoys suffering, then there is no reason not to indulge him in his wont.

The term "sadist" in popular usage describes one who obtains pleasure from indiscriminate brutality. Actually, though, a *true* sadist is selective. He carefully chooses from the vast reserve of appropriate victims, and takes great delight in giving those who thrive on misery the fulfillment of their desires. The "well-adjusted" sadist is epicurean in selecting those on whom his energies will be well-spent! If a person is healthy enough to admit he is a masochist and enjoys being enslaved and whipped, the real sadist is glad to oblige!

Aside from the foregoing exceptions, the Satanist would not intentionally hurt others by violating their sexual rights. If you attempt to impose your sexual desires upon others who do not welcome your advances, you are infringing upon *their* sexual freedom. Therefore, Satanism *does not* advocate rape, child molesting, sexual defilement of animals, or any other form of sexual activity which entails the participation of those who are unwilling or whose innocence or naïveté would allow them to be intimidated or misguided into doing something against their wishes.

If all parties involved are mature adults who willingly take full responsibility for their actions and voluntarily engage in a given form of sexual expression—*even if it is generally considered taboo*—then there is no reason for them to repress their sexual inclinations.

If you are aware of all the implications, advantages, and disadvantages, and are certain your actions will hurt no one who does not wish or deserve to be hurt, you have no cause to suppress your sexual preferences.

Just as no two people are exactly the same in their choice of diet or have the same capacity for the consumption of food, sexual tastes and appetites vary from person to person. No person or society has the right to set limitations on the sexual standards or the frequency of sexual activity of another. Proper sexual conduct can only be judged within the context of each individual situation. Therefore, what one person considers sexually correct and moral may be frustrating to another. The reverse is also true; one person may have great sexual prowess, but it is unjust for him to belittle another whose sexual capacity may not equal his own, and inconsiderate for him to impose himself upon the other person, i.e., the man who has a voracious sexual appetite, but whose wife's sexual needs do not match his own. It is unfair for him to expect her to enthusiastically respond to his overtures; but she must display the same degree of thoughtfulness. In the instances when she does not feel great passion, she should either passively, but *pleasantly*, accept him sexually, or raise no complaint if he chooses to find his needed release elsewhere—including auto-erotic practices.

The ideal relationship is one in which the people are deeply in love with one another and are sexually compatible. However, perfect relationships are relatively uncommon. It is important to point out here that spiritual love and sexual love can, but do not necessarily, go hand in hand. If there is a certain amount of sexual compatibility, often it is limited; and some, but not all, of the sexual desires will be fulfilled.

There is no greater sexual pleasure than that derived from association with someone you deeply love, *if* you are sexually well-suited. If you are not suited to one another sexually, though, it must be stressed that lack of sexual compatibility does not indicate lack of spiritual love. One can, and often does, exist without the other. As a matter of fact, often one member of a couple will resort to outside sexual activity *because* he deeply loves his mate, and wishes to avoid hurting or imposing upon his loved one. Deep spiritual love is enriched by sexual love, and it is certainly a necessary ingredient for any satisfactory relationship; but because of differing sexual predilections, outside sexual activity or masturbation sometimes provides a needed supplement.

Masturbation, considered a sexual taboo by many people, creates a guilt problem not easily dealt with. Much emphasis must be placed on this subject, as it constitutes an extremely important ingredient of many a successful magical working.

Ever since the Judaeo-Christian Bible described the sin of Onan (Gen. 38:7-10), man has considered the seriousness and consequences of the "solitary vice." Even though modern sexologists have explained the sin of Onan as simply *coitus interruptus*, the damage has been done through centuries of theological misinterpretation.

Aside from actual sex crimes, masturbation is one of the most frowned upon sexual acts. During the last century, innumerable texts were written describing the horrific consequences of masturbation. Practically all physical or mental illnesses were

71

attributed to the evils of masturbation. Pallor of the complexion, shortness of breath, furtive expression, sunken chest, nervousness, pimples and loss of appetite are only a few of the many characteristics supposedly resulting from masturbation; total physical and mental collapse was assured if one did not heed the warnings in those handbooks for young men.

The lurid descriptions in such texts would be almost humorous, were it not for the unhappy fact that even though contemporary sexologists, doctors, writers, etc. have done much to remove the stigma of masturbation, the deep-seated guilts induced by the nonsense in those sexual primers have been only partially erased. A large percentage of people, especially those over forty, cannot emotionally accept the fact that masturbation is natural and healthy, even if they now accept it intellectually; and they, in turn, relate their repugnance, often subconsciously, to their children.

It was thought that one would go insane if, despite numerous admonitions, his auto-erotic practices persisted. This preposterous myth grew from reports of wide-spread masturbation by the inmates of mental institutions. It was assumed that since almost all incurably insane people masturbated, it was their masturbation that had driven them mad. No one ever stopped to consider that the lack of sexual partners of the opposite sex and the freedom from inhibition, which is a characteristic of extreme insanity, were the real reasons for the masturbatory practices of the insane.

Many people would *rather* have their mates seek outside sexual activity than perform auto-erotic acts because of their own guilt feelings, the mate's repugnance towards having them engage in masturbation, or the *fear* of their mate's repugnance—although in a surprising number of cases, a vicarious thrill is obtained from the knowledge that the mate is having sexual experiences with outsiders—although this is seldom admitted.

If stimulation *is* provided by envisioning one's mate sexually engaged with others, this should be brought out into the open where both parties may gain from such activities. However, if the prohibition of masturbation is only due to guilt feelings on the part of one or both parties, they should make every attempt to erase those guilts—or utilize them. Many relationships might be saved from destruction if the people involved did not feel guilt about performing the *natural* act of masturbation.

Masturbation is regarded as evil because it produces pleasure derived from intentionally fondling a "forbidden" area of the body by one's own hand. The guilt feelings accompanying most sexual acts can be assuaged by the religiously-acceptable contention that your sensual delights are necessary to produce off-spring—even though you cautiously watch the calendar for the "safe" days. You cannot, however, placate yourself with this rationale while engaging in masturbatory practices.

No matter what you've been told about the "immaculate conception"—even if blind faith allows you to swallow this absurdity—you know full well if *you* are to produce a child, there must be sexual contact with a person of the opposite sex! If you feel guilty for committing the "original sin," you certainly will feel even deeper guilt for performing a sex act *only* for self-gratification, with no intention of creating children.

The Satanist fully realizes why religionists declare masturbation to be sinful. Like all other natural acts people *will* do it, no matter how severely reprimanded. Causing guilt is an important facet of their malicious scheme to obligate people to atone for "sins" by paying the mortgages on temples of abstinence!

Even if a person is no longer struggling under the burden of religiously-induced guilt (or thinks he isn't), modern man still feels shame if he yields to his masturbatory desires. A man may feel robbed of his masculinity if he satisfies himself auto-erotically rather than engaging in the competitive game of woman chasing. A woman may satisfy herself sexually but yearns for the ego-gratification that comes from the sport of seduction. Neither the quasi Casanova nor bogus vamp feels adequate when "reduced" to masturbation for sexual gratification; both would prefer even an inadequate partner. Satanically speaking, though, it is far better to engage in a perfect fantasy

73

than to cooperate in an unrewarding experience with another person. With masturbation, you are in complete control of the situation.

To illustrate the undebatable fact that masturbation is an entirely normal and healthy practice: it is performed by all members of the animal kingdom. Human children will also follow their instinctive masturbatory desires, *unless* they have been scolded for it by their indignant parents, who were undoubtably berated for it by *their* parents, and so on down the retrocedent line.

It is unfortunate, but true, that the sexual guilts of parents will immutably be passed on to their children. In order to save our children from the ill-fated sexual destiny of our parents, grandparents, and possibly ourselves, the perverted moral code of the past must be exposed for what it is: a pragmatically organized set of rules which, if rigidly obeyed, would destroy us! Unless we emancipate ourselves from the ridiculous sexual standards of our present society, including the so-called sexual revolution, the neuroses caused by those stifling regulations will persist. Adherence to the sensible and humanistic new morality of Satanism can—and will—evolve society in which our children can grow up healthy and without the devastating moral encumbrances of our existing sick society.

NOT ALL VAMPIRES
SUCK BLOOD!

SATANISM represents responsibility to the responsible, instead of concern for psychic vampires.

Many people who walk the earth practice the fine art of making others feel responsible and even indebted to them, without cause. Satanism observes these leeches in their true light. Psychic vampires are individuals who drain others of their vital energy. This type of person can be found in all avenues of society. They fill no useful purpose in our lives, and are neither love objects nor *true* friends. Yet we feel responsible to the psychic vampire without knowing why.

If you think you may be the victim of such a person, there are a few simple rules which will help you form a decision. Is there a person you often call or visit, even though you really don't want to, because you know you will feel guilty if you don't? Or, do you find yourself constantly doing favors for one who doesn't come forward and ask, but hints? Often the psychic vampire will use reverse psychology, saying: "Oh, I couldn't ask you to do that"—and you, in turn, insist upon doing it. The psychic vampire *never* demands anything of you. That would be far too presumptuous. They simply let their wishes be known in subtle ways which will prevent them from being considered pests. They "wouldn't think of imposing" and are always content to willingly accept their lot, without the slightest complaint—outwardly!

Their sins are not of commission, but of omission. It's what they *don't* say, not what they *do* say, that makes you feel you must account to them. They are much too crafty to make overt demands upon you, because they know you would resent it, and would have a tangible and legitimate reason for denying them.

A large percentage of these people have special "attributes" which make their dependence upon you more feasible and much more effective. Many psychic vampires are invalids (or pretend to be) or are "mentally or emotionally disturbed." Others might feign ignorance or incompetence so you will, out of pity—or more often, exasperation—do things for them.

The traditional way to banish a demon or elemental is to recognize it for what it is, and exorcise it. Recognition of these modern-day demons and their methods is the only antidote for their devastating hold over you.

Most people accept these passively vicious individuals at face value only because their insidious maneuvers have never been pointed out to them. They merely accept these "poor souls" as being less fortunate than themselves, and feel they must help them however they can. It is this misdirected sense of responsibility (or unfounded sense of guilt) which nourishes well the "altruisms" upon which these parasites feast!

The psychic vampire is allowed to exist because he cleverly chooses conscientious, responsible people for his victims—people with great dedication to their "moral obligations."

In some cases we are vampirized by groups of people, as well as individuals. Every fund raising organization, be it a charitable foundation, community council, religious or fraternal association, etc., carefully selects a person who is adept at making others feel guilty for its chairman or coordinator. It is the job of this chairman to intimidate us into opening first our hearts, and then our wallets, to the recipient of their "good will" —never mentioning that, in many cases, *their* time is not unselfishly donated, but that they are drawing a fat salary for their "noble deeds." They are masters at playing upon the sympathy and consideration of responsible people. How often we see little children who have been sent forth by these self-righteous Fagins to painlessly extract donations from the kindly. Who can resist the innocent charm of a child?

There are, of course, people who are not happy unless they are giving, but many of us do not fit into this category. Unfortunately, we are often put upon to do things we do not genuinely feel should be required of us. A conscientious person finds it very difficult to decide between voluntary and imposed charity. He wants to do what is right and just, and finds it perplexing trying to decide exactly who he should help and what degree of aid should *rightfully* be expected of him.

Each person must decide for himself what his obligations are to his respective friends, family, and community. Before donating his time and money to those outside his immediate family and close circle of friends, he must decide what he can afford, without depriving those closest to him. When taking these things into consideration he must be certain to include *himself* among those who mean most to him. He must carefully evaluate the validity of the request and the personality or motives of the person asking it of him.

It is extremely difficult for a person to learn to say "no" when all his life he has said "yes." But unless he wants to be constantly taken advantage of, he *must* learn to say "no" when circumstances justify doing so. If you allow them, psychic vampires will gradually infiltrate your everyday life until you have no privacy left—and your constant feeling of concern for them will deplete you of all ambition.

A psychic vampire will always select a person who is relatively content and satisfied with his life—a person who is happily married, pleased with his job, and generally well-adjusted to the world around him—to feed upon. The very fact that the psychic vampire chooses to victimize a happy person shows that he is lacking all the things his victim has; he will do everything he can to stir up trouble and disharmony between his victim and those people he holds dear.

Therefore, be wary of anyone who seems to have no real friends and no appearant interest in life (except you). He will usually tell you he is very selective in his choice of friends, or doesn't make friends easily because of the high standards he sets for his companions. (To acquire *and keep* friends, one must be willing to give of himself—something of which the psychic vampire is incapable.) But he will hasten to add that *you* fulfill every requirement and are truly an outstanding exception among men—*you* are one of the very few worthy of his friendship.

Lest you confuse desperate love (which is a very selfish thing) with psychic vampirism, the vast difference between the two must be clarified. The only way to determine if you are being vampirized is to weigh what you give the person compared to what they give you in return.

You may, at times, become annoyed by the obligations put upon you by a loved one, a close friend, or even an employer. But before you label them psychic vampires, you must ask yourself, "What am I getting in return?" If your spouse or lover insists that you call them frequently, but you also require them to account to you for their time spent away from you, you must realize this is a give and take situation. Or, if a friend is in the habit of calling upon you for help at inopportune moments, but you similarly depend upon them to give your immediate needs priority, you must regard it as a fair exchange. If your employer asks you to do a little more than is normally expected of you in your particular position, but will overlook occasional tardiness or will give you time off when you need it, you certainly have no cause for complaint and need not feel he is taking advantage of you.

You are, however, being vampirized if you are incessantly called upon or expected to do favors for someone who, when you need a favor, always happens to have other "pressing obligations."

Many psychic vampires will give you material things for the express purpose of making you feel you owe them something in return, thereby binding you to them. The difference between your giving, and theirs, is that your return payment must come in a non-material form. They want you to feel obligated to them, and would be very disappointed and even resentful if you attempted to repay them with material objects. In essence, you have "sold your soul" to them, and they'll constantly remind you of your duty to them, by *not* reminding you.

Being purely Satanic, the only way to deal with a psychic vampire is to "play dumb" and act as though they are *genuinely* altruistic and *really* expect nothing in return. Teach them a lesson by *graciously* taking what they give you, thanking them loudly enough for all to hear, and walking away! In this way you come out the victor. What can they say? And when you are inevitably expected to repay their "generosity," (this is the hard part!) you say "NO"—but again, *graciously!* When they feel you falling from their clutches two things will happen. First, they will act "crushed," hoping your old feeling of duty and sympathy will return, and when (and if) it doesn't, they will show their *true* colors and will become angry and vindictive.

Once you have moved them to this point, YOU can play the role of the injured party. After all, you've done nothing wrong—you just happened to have had "pressing obligations" when they needed you, and since nothing was expected in return for their gifts, there should be no hard feelings.

Generally, the psychic vampire will realize his methods have been discovered and will not press the issue. He will not continue to waste his time with you, but will move on to his next unsuspecting victim.

There are times, however, when the psychic vampire will not release his hold so easily, and will do everything possible to torment you. They have plenty of time for this because, when once rejected, they will neglect all else (what little else they have, that is) to devote their every waking moment to planning the revenge to which they feel they are entitled. For this reason, it is best to avoid a relationship with this kind of person in the first place. Their "adulation" and dependence upon you may, at first, be very flattering, and their material gifts very attractive, but you will eventually find yourself paying for them many times over.

Don't waste your time with people who will ultimately destroy you, but concentrate instead on those who will appreciate your responsibility to them, and, likewise, feel responsible to you.

And if *you* are a psychic vampire—take heed! Beware of the Satanist—he is ready and willing to gleefully drive the proverbial stake through your heart!

INDULGENCE . . . *NOT* COMPULSION

THE HIGHEST PLATEAU OF HUMAN DEVELOPMENT
IS THE AWARENESS OF THE FLESH!

SATANISM encourages its followers to indulge in their natural desires. Only by so doing can you be a completely satisfied person with no frustrations which can be harmful to yourself and others around you. Therefore, the most simplified description of the Satanic belief is:

INDULGENCE INSTEAD OF ABSTINENCE

People often mistake compulsion for indulgence, but there is a world of difference between the two. A compulsion is never created by indulging, but by not being able to indulge. By making something taboo, it only serves to intensify the desire. Everyone likes to do the things they have been told not to. "Forbidden fruits are sweetest."

Webster's Encyclopedic Dictionary defines *indulgence* thusly: "To give oneself up to; not to restrain or oppose; to give free course to; to gratify by compliance; to yield to." The dictionary definition of *compulsion* is: "The act of compelling or driving by force, physical or moral; constraint of the will; (compulsory, obligatory)." In other words, indulgence implies choice, whereas compulsion indicates the lack of choice.

When a person has no proper release for his desires they rapidly build up and become compulsions. If everyone had a particular time and place for the purpose of periodically indulging in their personal desires, without fear of embarrassment or reproach, they would be sufficiently released to lead unfrustrated lives in the everyday world. They would be free to plunge headlong into whatever undertaking they might choose instead of going about their duties half-heartedly, their creative urges frustrated by denying their natural desires. This would apply in the majority of cases, but there will always be those who work better under pressure.

Generally, those who need to endure a certain amount of hardship to produce to their full capabilities are in basically artistic vocations. (More will be said later about fulfillment through self-denial.) This does not mean to imply that all artists fit into this category. On the contrary, many artists are unable to produce unless their basic animal needs have been satisfied.

For the most part, it is not the artist or individualist, but the average middle-class working man or woman who is lacking the proper release for their desires. It is ironic that the responsible, respectable person—the one who pays society's bills—should be the one given the least in return. It is he who must be ever conscious of his "moral obligations," and who is condemned for normally indulging in his *natural* desires.

The Satanic religion considers this a gross injustice. He who upholds his responsibilities should be most entitled to the pleasures of his choice, without censure from the society *he* serves.

Finally a religion (Satanism) has been formed which commends and rewards those who support the society in which they live, instead of denouncing them for their human needs.

From every set of principles (be it religious, political, or philosophical), some good can be extracted. Amidst the madness of the Hitlerian concept, one point stands out as a shining example of this—"strength through joy!" Hitler was no fool when he offered the German people happiness, *on a personal level*, to insure their loyalty to him, and peak efficiency from them.

It has been clearly established that the majority of all illnesses are of a psychosomatic nature, and that psychosomatic illnesses are a direct result of frustration. It has been said that "the good die young." The good, by Christian standards, *do*

82

die young. It is the frustration of our natural instincts which leads to the premature deterioration of our minds and bodies.

It has become very fashionable to concentrate on the betterment of the mind and spirit, and to consider giving pleasure to one's body (the very shell without which the mind and spirit could not exist) to be coarse, crude, and unrefined. AS OF LATE, MOST PEOPLE WHO DEEM THEMSELVES EMANCIPATED HAVE LEFT NORMALCY ONLY TO "TRANSCEND" INTO IDIOCY! By way of bending their behinds around to meet their navels, subsisting on wild and exotic diets like brown rice and tea, they feel they will arrive at a great state of spiritual development.

"Hogwash!" says the Satanist. He would rather eat a good hearty meal, exercise his imagination, and transcend by means of physical and emotional fulfillment. It seems, to the Satanist, that after being harnessed with unreasonable religious demands for so many centuries, one would welcome the chance to be human for once!

If anyone thinks that by denying his natural desires he can avoid mediocrity, he should examine the Eastern mystical beliefs which have been in great intellectual favor in recent years. Christianity is "old hat," so those who wish to escape its fetters have turned to so-called enlightened religions, such as Buddhism. Although Christianity is certainly deserving of the criticism it has received, perhaps it has been taking more than its share of the blame. The followers of the mystical beliefs are every bit as guilty of the little humanisms as the "misguided" Christians. Both religions are based on trite philosophies, but the mystical religionists profess to be enlightened and emancipated from the guilt-ridden dogma which is typified by Christianity. However, the Eastern mystic is even more preoccupied than the Christian with avoiding animalistic actions that remind him he is not a "saint," but merely a man—only another form of animal, sometimes better, *more often worse*, than those who walk on all fours; and who, because of his "divine spiritual and intellectual development," has become the most vicious animal of all!

The Satanist asks, "What is wrong with being human, and

83

having human limitations as well as assets?" By denying his desires the mystic has come no closer to overcoming compulsion than his kindred soul, the Christian. The Eastern mystical beliefs have taught people to contemplate their navels, stand on their heads, stare at blank walls, avoid the use of labels in life, and discipline themselves against any desire for materialistic pleasure. Nevertheless, I am sure you have seen just as many so-called disciplined yogis with the inability to control a smoking habit as anyone else; or just as many supposedly emancipated Buddhists become just as excited as a "less aware" person when they are confronted with a member of the opposite—or in some cases, the same—sex. Yet when asked to explain the reason for their hypocrisy, these people retreat into the ambiguousness which characterizes their faith—no one can pin them down if there are no straight answers that can be given!

The simple fact of the matter is that the very thing which has led this type of person to a faith which preaches abstinence, is *indulgence*. Their compulsive masochism is the reason for choosing a religion which not only advocates self-denial, but praises them for it; and gives them a sacrosanct avenue of expression for their masochistic needs. The more abuse they can stand, the holier they become.

Masochism, to most people, represents a rejection of indulgence. Satanism points out many meanings behind the meanings, and considers masochism to be an *indulgence* if any attempt to sway or change the person from his masochistic traits is met with resentment and/or failure. The Satanist does not condemn these people for giving vent to their masochistic desires, but he *does* feel the utmost contempt towards those who cannot be honest enough (at least with themselves) to face and accept their masochism as a natural part of their personality make-up.

Having to use religion as an excuse for their masochism is bad enough, but these people actually have the effrontery to feel *superior* to those who are not bound-up in self-deceitful expression of their fetishes! These people would be the first to condemn a man who found his weekly release with a person who would beat him soundly, thereby releasing himself from the very thing which would, if unreleased, make him—as they are—a compulsive church-goer or religious fanatic. By finding adequate release for his masochistic desires, he no longer needs to debase and deny himself in his every waking moment, as do these compulsive masochists.

Satanists are encouraged to indulge in the seven deadly sins, as they need hurt no one; they were only invented by the Christian Church to insure guilt on the part of its followers. The Christian Church knows that it is impossible for anyone to avoid committing these sins, as they are all things which we, being human, most naturally do. After inevitably committing these sins financial offerings to the church in order to "pay off" God are employed as a sop to the parishioner's conscience!

Satan has never needed a book of rules, because vital natural forces have kept man "sinful" and intent on preserving himself and his feelings. Nevertheless, demoralizing attempts have been made on his body and being for his "soul's" sake, which only illustrate how misconceived and misused the labels of "indulgence" versus "compulsion" have become.

Sexual activity certainly *is* condoned and encouraged by Satanism, but obviously the fact that it is the only religion which honestly takes this stand, is the reason it has been traditionally given so much literary space.

Naturally, if most people belong to religions which repress them sexually, anything written on this provocative subject is going to make for titillating reading.

If all attempts to sell something (be it a product or an idea) have failed—sex will always sell it. The reason for this is that even though people now *consciously* accept sex as a normal and necessary function, their *subconscious* is still bound by the taboo which religion has placed upon it. So, again, what is denied is more intensely desired. It is this bugaboo regarding sex which causes the literature devoted to the Satanic views on the subject to overshadow all else written about Satanism.

The *true* Satanist is not mastered by sex any more than he is mastered by any of his other desires. As with all other pleasurable things, the Satanist is master *of*, rather than mastered *by* sex. He is not the perverted fiend who is just waiting for the opportunity to deflower every young virgin, nor is he the skulking degenerate who furtively hangs around the "dirty" bookstores, slavering over the "nasty" pictures. If pornography fills his needs for the moment, he unashamedly buys some "choice items" and guiltlessly peruses them at his leisure.

"We have to accept the fact that man has become disgruntled at being constantly repressed, but we must do everything we can to at least temper the sinful desires of man, lest they run rampant in this new age," say the religionists of the right-hand path to the questioning Satanist. "Why continue to think of these desires as shameful and something to be repressed, if you now admit they are natural?" returns the Satanist. Could it be that the white-light religionists are a bit "sour-grapes" about the fact that they didn't think of a religion, before the Satanists, which would be enjoyable to follow; and if the truth were known, would they too not like to have a bit more pleasure out of life, but for fear of losing face, cannot admit it? Could it also be that they are afraid people will, after hearing about Satanism, tell themselves "This is for me—why should I continue with a religion which condemns me for everything I do, even though there is nothing actually wrong with it?" The Satanist thinks this is more than likely true.

There is certainly much evidence that past religions are, every day, lifting more and more of their ridiculous restrictions. Even so, when an entire religion is based on abstinence instead of indulgence (as it should be) there is little left when it has been revised to meet the current needs of man. So, why waste time "buying oats for a dead horse"?

The watchword of Satanism is INDULGENCE instead of "abstinence" . . . BUT—it is *not* "compulsion."

ON THE CHOICE
OF
A HUMAN SACRIFICE

THE supposed purpose in performing the ritual of sacrifice is to throw the energy provided by the blood of the freshly slaughtered victim into the atmosphere of the magical working, thereby intensifying the magician's chances of success.

The "white" magician assumes that since blood represents the life force, there is no better way to appease the gods or demons than to present them with suitable quantities of it. Combine this rationale with the fact that a dying creature is expending an overabundance of adrenal and other biochemical energies, and you have what appears to be an unbeatable combination.

The "white" magician, wary of the consequences involved in the killing of a human being, naturally utilizes birds, or other "lower" creatures in his ceremonies. It seems these sanctimonious wretches feel no guilt in the taking of a non-human life, as opposed to a human's.

The fact of the matter is that if the "magician" is worthy of his name, he will be uninhibited enough to release the necessary force *from his own body,* instead of from an unwilling and undeserving victim!

Contrary to all established magical theory, the release of this force is NOT effected in the actual spilling of blood, *but in the death throes of the living creature!* This discharge of bioelectrical energy is the very same phenomenon which occurs during any profound heightening of the emotions, such as: sexual orgasm, blind anger, mortal terror, consuming grief, etc. Of these emotions, the easiest entered into of one's own volition are sexual orgasm and anger, with grief running a close third. Remembering that the two most readily available of these three (sexual orgasm and anger) have been burned into man's unconscious as "sinful" by religionists, it is small wonder they are shunned by the "white" magician, who plods along carrying the greatest of all millstones of guilt!

The inhibitive and asinine absurdity in the need to kill an innocent living creature at the high-point of a ritual, as practiced by erstwhile "wizards," is obviously their "lesser of the evils" when a discharge of energy is called for. These poor conscience-stricken fools, who have been calling themselves witches and warlocks, would sooner chop the head off a goat or chicken in an attempt to harness its death agony, than have the "blasphemous" bravery to masturbate in full view of the Jehovah whom they claim to deny! The only way these mystical cowards can ritualistically release themselves is through the agony of another's death (actually their own, by proxy) rather than the indulgent force which *produces* life! The treaders of the path of white light are truly the cold and the dead! No wonder these tittering pustules of "mystic wisdom" must stand within protective circles and bind the "evil" forces in order to keep themselves "safe" from attack—ONE GOOD ORGASM WOULD PROBABLY KILL THEM!

The use of a human sacrifice in a Satanic ritual does not imply that the sacrifice is slaughtered "to appease the gods." *Symbolically*, the victim is destroyed through the working of a hex or curse, which in turn leads to the physical, mental or emotional destruction of the "sacrifice" in ways and means not attributable to the magician.

The only time a Satanist would perform a human sacrifice would be if it were to serve a two-fold purpose; that being to release the magician's wrath in the throwing of a curse, and more important, to dispose of a totally obnoxious and deserving individual.

Under NO circumstances would a Satanist sacrifice any animal or baby! For centuries, propagandists of the right-hand path have been prattling over the supposed sacrifices of small children and voluptuous maidens at the hands of diabolists. It would be thought that anyone reading or hearing of these heinous accounts would immediately question their authenticity, taking into consideration the biased sources of the stories. On the contrary, as with all "holy" lies which are accepted without reservation, this assumed modus operandi of the Satanists persists to this day!

There are sound and logical reasons why the Satanists could *not* perform such sacrifices. Man, the animal, is the godhead to the Satanist. The purest form of carnal existence reposes in the bodies of animals and human children who have not grown old enough to deny themselves their natural desires. They can perceive things that the average adult human can never hope to. Therefore, the Satanist holds these beings in a sacred regard, knowing he can learn much from these natural magicians of the world.

The Satanist is aware of the universal custom of the treader of the path of Agarthi; the killing of the god. Inasmuch as gods are always created in man's own image—and the average man hates what he sees in himself—the inevitable must occur: the sacrifice of the god who represents himself. The Satanist does *not* hate himself, nor the gods he might choose, and has no desire to destroy himself or anything for which he stands! It is for this reason he could never willfully harm an animal or child.

The question arises, "Who, then, would be considered a fit and proper human sacrifice, and how is one qualified to pass judgment on such a person?" The answer is brutally simple. Anyone who has unjustly wronged you—one who has "gone out of his way" to hurt you—to deliberately cause trouble and hardship for you or those dear to you. In short, a person asking to be cursed by their very actions.

When a person, by his reprehensible behavior, practically

cries out to be destroyed, it is truly your moral obligation to indulge them their wish. The person who takes every opportunity to "pick on" others is often mistakenly called "sadistic." In reality, this person is a misdirected masochist who is working towards his own destruction. The reason a person viciously strikes out against you is because they are afraid of you or what you represent, or are resentful of your happiness. They are weak, insecure, and on extremely shaky ground when you throw your curse, and they make ideal human sacrifices.

It is sometimes easy to overlook the actual wrongdoing of the victim of your curse, when one considers how "unhappy" a person he really is. It is not so easy, though, to retrace the damaging footsteps of your antagonist and make right those practical situations he or she has made wrong.

The "ideal sacrifice" may be emotionally insecure, but nonetheless can, in the machinations of his insecurity, cause severe damage to *your* tranquility or sound reputation. "Mental illness," "nervous breakdown," "maladjustment," "anxiety neuroses," "broken homes," "sibling rivalry," etc., etc., ad infinitum have too long been convenient excuses for vicious and irresponsible actions. Anyone who says "we must try to understand" those who make life miserable for those undeserving of misery is aiding and abetting a social cancer! The apologists for these rabid humans deserve any clobberings they get at the hands of their charges!

Mad dogs are destroyed, and *they* need help far more than the human who conveniently froths at the mouth when irrational behavior is in order! It is easy to say, "So what!— these people are insecure, so they can't hurt me." But the fact remains—*given the opportunity they would destroy you!*

Therefore, you have every right to (symbolically) destroy them, and if your curse provokes their actual annihilation, rejoice that you have been instrumental in ridding the world of a pest! If your success or happiness disturbs a person—you owe him *nothing!* He is made to be trampled under foot! IF PEOPLE HAD TO TAKE THE CONSEQUENCES OF THEIR OWN ACTIONS, THEY WOULD THINK TWICE!

LIFE AFTER DEATH
THROUGH FULFILLMENT
OF THE EGO

MAN is aware that he will die, someday. Other animals, when nearing death, know they are about to die; but it is not until death is certain that the animal senses his coming departure from this world. And even then he does not know exactly what is entailed in dying. It is often pointed out that animals accept death gracefully, without fear or resistance. This is a beautiful concept, but one that only holds true in cases where death for the animal is unavoidable.

When an animal is sick or injured he will fight for his life with every ounce of strength he has left. It is this unshakable will to live that, if man were not so "highly evolved," would also give him the fighting spirit he needs to stay alive.

It is a well known fact that many people die simply because they give up and just don't care anymore. This is understandable if the person is very ill, with no apparent chance for recovery. But this often is not the case. Man has become lazy. He has learned to take the easy way out. Even suicide has become less repugnant to many people than any number of other sins. Religion is totally to blame for this.

Death, in most religions, is touted as a great spiritual awakening—one which is prepared for throughout life. This concept is very appealing to one who has not had a satisfactory life; but to those who have experienced all the joys life has to offer, there is a great dread attached to dying. This is as it should be. It is this lust for life which will allow the vital person to live on after the inevitable death of his fleshly shell.

History shows that men who have given their own lives in pursuit of an ideal have been deified for their martyrdom. Religionists and political leaders have been very crafty in laying their plans. By holding the martyr up as a shining example to his fellow men, they eliminate the common sense reaction that willful self-destruction goes against all animal logic. To the Satanist, martyrdom and non-personalized heroism is to be associated not with integrity, but with stupidity. This, of course, does not apply in situations which involve the safety of a loved one. But to give one's own life for something as impersonal as a political or religious issue is the ultimate in masochism.

Life is the one great indulgence; death the one great abstinence. To a person who is satisfied with his earthly existence, life is like a party; and no one likes to leave a *good* party. By the same token, if a person is enjoying himself here on earth he will not so readily give up this life for the promise of an afterlife about which he knows nothing.

The Eastern mystical beliefs teach humans to discipline themselves against any conscious will for success so they might dissolve themselves into "Universal Cosmic Awareness"—anything to avoid good healthy self-satisfaction or honest pride in earthly accomplishments!

It is interesting to note that the areas in which this type of belief flourishes are those where material gains are not easily obtainable. For this reason the predominant religious belief must be one which commends its followers for their rejection of material things and their avoidance of the use of labels which attaches a certain amount of importance to material gains. In this way the people can be pacified into accepting their lot, no matter how small it may be.

Satanism uses many labels. If it were not for names, very few of us would understand anything in life, much less attach any significance to it;—and significance compels recognition, which is something *everyone* wants, especially the Eastern mystic who tries to prove to everyone how he can meditate longer or stand more deprivation and pain than the next fellow.

The Eastern philosophies preach the dissolution of man's ego before he can produce sins. It is unfathomable to the Satanist to conceive of an ego which would willfully choose denial of itself.

In countries where this is used as a sop for the willingly impoverished, it is understandable that a philosophy which teaches the denial of the ego would serve a useful purpose— at least for those in power, to whom it would be detrimental if their people were discontented. But for anyone who has every opportunity for material gain, to *choose* this form of religious thought seems foolish, indeed!

The Eastern mystic believes strongly in reincarnation. To a person who has virtually nothing in this life, the possibility that he may have been a king in a past life or may be one in the next life is very attractive, and does much to appease his need for self-respect. If there is nothing in which they can take pride in this life, they can console themselves by thinking, "there are always future lives." It never occurs to the believer in reincarnation that if his father, grandfather, and great-grandfather, etc. had developed "good karmas," by their adherence to the same beliefs and ethics as his present ones—then why is he now living in privation, rather than like a maharajah?

Belief in reincarnation provides a beautiful fantasy world in which a person can find the proper avenue of ego-expression, but at the same time claim to have dissolved his ego. This is emphasized by the roles people choose for themselves in their past or future lives.

Believers in reincarnation do not always choose an honorable character. If the person is of a highly respectable and conservative nature, he will often choose a colorful rogue or gangster, thereby fulfilling his alter-ego. Or, a woman who has much social status may pick a harlot or famous courtesan for the characterization of herself in a past life.

If people were able to divorce themselves from the stigma

attached to personal ego-fulfillment, they would not need to play self-deceitful games such as belief in reincarnation as a means of satisfying their natural need for ego-fulfillment.

The Satanist believes in complete gratification of his ego. Satanism, in fact, is the *only* religion which advocates the intensification or encouragement of the ego. Only if a person's own ego is sufficiently fulfilled, can he afford to be kind and complimentary to others, without robbing himself of his self-respect. We generally think of a braggart as a person with a large ego; in reality, his bragging results from a need to satisfy his impoverished ego.

Religionists have kept their followers in line by suppressing their egos. By making their followers feel inferior, the awesomeness of their god is insured. Satanism encourages its members to develop a good strong ego because it gives them the self-respect necessary for a vital existence in this life.

If a person has been vital throughout his life and has fought to the end for his earthly existence, it is this ego which will refuse to die, even after the expiration of the flesh which housed it. Young children are to be admired for their driving enthusiasm for life. This is exemplified by the small child who refuses to go to bed when there is something exciting going on, and when once put to bed, will sneak down the stairs to peek through the curtain and watch. It is this child-like vitality that will allow the Satanist to peek through the curtain of darkness and death and remain earthbound.

Self-sacrifice is not encouraged by the Satanic religion. Therefore, unless death comes as an indulgence because of extreme circumstances which make the termination of life a welcome relief from an unendurable earthly existence, suicide is frowned upon by the Satanic religion.

Religious martyrs have taken their own lives, not because life was intolerable for them, but to use their supreme sacrifice as a tool to further the religious belief. We must assume, then, that suicide, if done for the sake of the church, is condoned and even encouraged—even though their scriptures label it a

94

sin—because religious martyrs of the past have always been deified.

It is rather curious that the only time suicide is considered sinful by other religions is when it comes as an indulgence.

RELIGIOUS HOLIDAYS

THE highest of all holidays in the Satanic religion is the date of one's own birth. This is in direct contradiction to the holy of holy days of other religions, which deify a particular god who has been created in an anthropomorphic form of their own image, thereby showing that the ego is not really buried.

The Satanist feels: "Why not really be honest and if you are going to create a god in your image, why not create that god as yourself." Every man is a god if he chooses to recognize himself as one. So, the Satanist celebrates his own birthday as the most important holiday of the year. After all, aren't you happier about the fact that you were born than you are about the birth of someone you have never even met? Or for that matter, aside from religious holidays, why pay higher tribute to the birthday of a president or to a date in history than we do to the day we were brought into this greatest of all worlds?

Despite the fact that some of us may not have been wanted, or at least were not particularly planned, we're glad, even if no one else is, that we're here! You should give yourself a pat on the back, buy yourself whatever you want, treat yourself like the king (or god) that you are, and generally celebrate your birthday with as much pomp and ceremony as possible.

After one's own birthday, the two major Satanic holidays are Walpurgisnacht and Halloween (or All Hallows' Eve).

St. Walpurgis—or Walpurga, or Walburga, depending

upon the time and area in which one is referring to her—was born in Sussex about the end of the Seventh or the beginning of the Eighth Century, and was educated at Winburn, Dorset, where after taking the veil, she remained for twenty-seven years. She then, at the insistence of her uncle, St. Boniface, and her brother, St. Wilibald, set out along with some other nuns to found religious houses in Germany. Her first settlement was at Bischofsheim in the diocese of Mainz, and two years later (754 A.D.) she became abbess of the Benedictine nunnery at Heidenheim, within her brother Wilibald's diocese of Eichstadt in Bavaria, where another brother, Winebald, had at the same time also been made head of a monastery. On the death of Winebald in 760 she succeeded him in his charge, retaining the superintendence of both houses until her death on February 25, 779. Her relics were translated to Eichstadt, where she was laid in a hollow rock, from which exuded a kind of bituminous oil, afterwards known as Walpurgis oil, regarded as having miraculous efficacy against disease. The cave became a place of pilgrimage, and a great church was built over the spot. She is commemorated at various times, but principally on May 1st, her day taking the place of an earlier Pagan festival. Amazingly enough, all of this rigmarole was found necessary simply to condone the continuance of the most important Pagan festival of the year—the grand climax of the spring equinox!

The Eve of May has been memorialized as the night that all of the demons, specters, afreets, and banshees would come forth and hold their wild revels, symbolizing the fruition of the spring equinox.

Halloween—All Hallows' Eve, or All Saints' Day—falls on October 31st or November 1st. Originally, All Hallows' Eve was one of the great fire festivals of Britain at the time of the Druids. In Scotland it was associated with the time when the spirits of the dead, the demons, witches, and sorcerers were unusually active and propitious. Paradoxically, All Hallows' Eve was also the night when young people performed magical rituals to determine their future marriage partners. The youth of the villages carried on with much merry-making and sensual revelry, but the older people took great care to safeguard their homes from the evil spirits, witches, and demons who had exceptional power that night.

The solstices and equinoxes are also celebrated as holidays, as they herald the first day of the seasons. The difference between a solstice and an equinox is a semantic one defining the relationship between the sun, moon, and the fixed stars. The solstice applies to summer and winter; the equinox refers to autumn and spring. The summer solstice is in June, and the winter solstice is in December. The autumn equinox is in September, and the spring equinox is in March. Both the equinoxes and the solstices vary a day or two from year to year, depending on the lunar cycle at the time, but usually fall on the 21st or 22nd of the month. Five to six weeks after these days the legendary Satanic revels are celebrated.

THE BLACK MASS

NO other single device has been associated with Satanism as much as the black mass. To say that the most blasphemous of all religious ceremonies is nothing more than a literary invention is certainly a statement which needs qualifying—but nothing could be truer.

The popular concept of the black mass is thus: a defrocked priest stands before an altar consisting of a nude woman, her legs spread-eagled and vagina thrust open, each of her outstretched fists grasping a black candle made from the fat of unbaptized babies, and a chalice containing the urine of a prostitute (or blood) reposing on her belly. An inverted cross hangs above the altar, and triangular hosts of ergot-laden bread or black-stained turnip are methodically blessed as the priest dutifully slips them in and out of the altar-lady's labia. Then, we are told, an invocation to Satan and various demons is followed by an array of prayers and psalms chanted backwards or interspersed with obscenities . . . all performed within the confines of a "protective" pentagram drawn on the floor. If the Devil appears he is invariably in the form of a rather eager man wearing the head of a black goat upon his shoulders. Then follows a potpourri of flagellation, prayer-book burning, cunnilingus, fellatio, and general hindquarters kissing —all done to a background of ribald recitations from the Holy Bible, and audible expectorations on the cross! If a baby can be slaughtered during the ritual, so much the better; for as everyone knows, this is the favorite sport of the Satanist!

If this sounds repugnant, then the success of the reports of the black mass, in keeping the devout in church, is easy to understand. No "decent" person could fail to side with the inquisitors when told of these blasphemies. The propagandists of the church did their job well, informing the public at one time or another of the heresies and heinous acts of the Pagans, Cathars, Bogomils, Templars and others who, because of their dualistic philosophies and sometimes Satanic logic, had to be eradicated.

The stories of unbaptized babies being stolen by Satanists for use in the mass were not only effective propaganda measures, but also provided a constant source of revenue for the Church, in the form of baptism fees. No Christian mother would, upon hearing of these diabolical kidnappings, refrain from getting her child properly baptized, post haste.

Another facet of man's nature was apparent in the fact that the writer or artist with lewd thoughts could exercise his most obscene predilections in the portrayal of the activities of heretics. The censor who views all pornography so that he will know what to warn others of is the modern equivalent of the medieval chronicler of the obscene deeds of the Satanists (and, of course, their modern journalistic counterparts). It is believed that the most complete library of pornography in the world is owned by the Vatican!

The kissing of the Devil's behind during the traditional black mass is easily recognized as the forerunner of the modern term used to describe one who will, through appealing to another's ego, gain materially from him. As all Satanic ceremonies were performed toward very real or material goals, the *oscularum infame* (or kiss of shame) was considered a symbolic requisite towards earthly, rather than spiritual, success.

The usual assumption is that the Satanic ceremony or service is always called a black mass. A black mass is *not* the magical ceremony practiced by Satanists. The Satanist would only employ the use of a black mass as a form of psychodrama. Furthermore, a black mass does not necessarily imply that the performers of such are Satanists. A black mass is essentially a parody on the religious service of the Roman Catholic Church, but can be loosely applied to a satire on any religious ceremony.

To the Satanist, the black mass, in its blaspheming of orthodox rites, is nothing more than a redundancy. The services of all established religions are actually parodies of old rituals performed by the worshippers of the earth and the flesh. In attempts to de-sexualize and de-humanize the Pagan beliefs, later men of spiritual faith whitewashed the honest meanings behind the rituals into the bland euphemisms now considered to be the "true mass." Even *if* the Satanist were to spend each night performing a black mass, he would no more be performing a travesty than the devout churchgoer who unwittingly attends his own "black mass"—*his* spoof on the honest and emotionally-sound rites of Pagan antiquity.

Any ceremony considered a black mass must effectively shock and outrage, as this seems to be the measure of its success. In the Middle Ages, blaspheming the holy church was shocking. Now, however, the Church does not present the awesome image it did during the inquisition. The traditional black mass is no longer the outrageous spectacle to the dilettante or renegade priest that it once was. If the Satanist wishes to create a ritual to blaspheme an accepted institution, for the purpose of psychodrama, he is careful to choose one that is not in vogue to parody. Thus, he is truly stepping on a sacred cow.

A black mass, today, would consist of the blaspheming of such "sacred" topics as Eastern mysticism, psychiatry, the psychedelic movement, ultra-liberalism, etc. Patriotism would be championed, drugs and their gurus would be defiled, acultural militants would be deified, and the decadence of ecclesiastical theologies might even be given a Satanic boost.

The Satanic magus has always been the catalyst for the dichotomy necessary in molding popular beliefs, and in this case a ceremony in the nature of a black mass may serve a far-reaching magical purpose.

In the year 1666, some rather interesting events occurred in France. With the death of François Mansart, the architect of the trapezoid, whose geometrics were to become the prototype

101

of the haunted house, the Palace of Versailles was being constructed, in accordance with his plans. The last of the glamorous priestesses of Satan, Jeanne-Marie Bouvier (Madame Guyon) was to be overshadowed by a shrewd opportunist and callous business-woman named Catherine Deshayes, otherwise known as LaVoisin. Here was an erstwhile beautician who, while dabbling in abortions and purveying the most efficient poisons to ladies desirous of eliminating unwanted husbands or lovers, found in the lurid accounts of the "messes noir" a proverbial brainstorm.

It is safe to say that 1666 was the year of the first "commercial" black mass! In the region south of St. Denis, which is now called LaGarenne, a great walled house was purchased by LaVoisin and fitted with dispensaries, cells, laboratories, and . . . a chapel. Soon it became de rigueur for royalty and lesser dilettantes to attend and participate in the very type of service mentioned earlier in this chapter. The organized fraud perpetrated in these ceremonies has become indelibly marked in history as the "true black mass."

When LaVoisin was arrested on March 13, 1679 (in the Church of Our Blessed Lady of Good Tidings, incidentally), the die had already been cast. The degraded activities of LaVoisin had stifled the majesty of Satanism for many years to come.

The Satanism-for-fun-and-games fad next appeared in England in the middle 18th Century in the form of Sir Francis Dashwood's Order of the Medmanham Franciscans, popularly called The Hell-Fire Club. While eliminating the blood, gore, and baby-fat candles of the previous century's masses, Sir Francis managed to conduct rituals replete with good dirty fun, and certainly provided a colorful and harmless form of psychodrama for many of the leading lights of the period. An interesting sideline of Sir Francis, which lends a clue to the climate of the Hell-Fire Club, was a group called the Dilettanti Club, of which he was the founder.

It was the 19th Century that brought a whitewashing to Satanism, in the feeble attempts of "white" magicians trying to perform "black" magic. This was a very paradoxical period for

Satanism, with writers such as Baudelaire and Huysmans who, despite their apparent obsession with evil, seemed nice enough fellows. The Devil developed his Luciferian personality for the public to see, and gradually evolved into a sort of drawing-room gentleman. This was the era of "experts" on the black arts, such as Eliphas Levi and countless trance-mediums who, with their carefully bound spirits and demons, have also succeeded in binding the minds of many who call themselves parapsychologists to this day!

As far as Satanism was concerned, the closest outward signs of this were the neo-Pagan rites conducted by MacGregor Mathers' Hermetic Order of the Golden Dawn, and Aleister Crowley's later Order of the Silver Star (A∴ A∴— Argentinum Astrum) and Order of Oriental Templars (O.T.O.),* which paranoiacally denied any association with Satanism, despite Crowley's self-imposed image of the beast of revelation. Aside from some rather charming poetry and a smattering of magical bric-a-brac, when not climbing mountains Crowley spent most of his time as a poseur par excellence and worked overtime to be wicked. Like his contemporary, Rev. (?) Montague Summers, Crowley obviously spent a large part of his life with his tongue jammed firmly into his cheek, but his followers, today, are somehow able to read esoteric meaning into his every word.

Perennially concurrent with these societies were the sex clubs using Satanism as a rationale—that persists today, for which tabloid newspaper writers may give thanks.

If it appears that the black mass developed from a literary invention of the church, to a depraved commercial actuality, to a psychodrama for dilettantes and iconoclasts, to an ace in the hole for popular media . . . then *where* does it fit into the true nature of Satanism—and *who* was practicing Satanic magic in those years beyond 1666?

The answer to this riddle lies in another. Is the person

---

* "Ordo Templi Orientis," Crowley's take-off on the German sect of the same name, originally founded in 1902, and practicing some of the principles set forth in this volume.

generally considered to be a Satanist really practicing Satanism *in its true sense,* or rather from the point of view taken by the opinion makers of heavenly persuasion? It has often been said, and rightly so, that all of the books about the Devil have been written by the agents of God. It is, therefore, quite easy to understand how a certain breed of devil worshippers was created through the inventions of theologians. This erstwhile "evil" character is not necessarily practicing *true* Satanism. Nor is he a living embodiment of the element of untrammeled pride or majesty of self which gave the post-Pagan world the church-man's definition of evil. He is instead the by-product of later and more elaborate propaganda.

The pseudo-Satanist has always managed to appear throughout modern history, with his black masses of varying degrees of blasphemy; but the *real* Satanist is not quite so easily recognized as such.

It would be an over-simplification to say that every success-ful man and woman on earth is, without knowing it, a practicing Satanist; but the thirst for earthly success and its ensuing realiza-tion are certainly grounds for Saint Peter turning thumbs down. If the rich man's entry into heaven seems as difficult as the camel's attempt to go through the eye of a needle; if the love of money is the root of all evil; then we must at least assume the most powerful men on earth to be the most Satanic. This applies to financiers, industrialists, popes, poets, dictators, and all assorted opinion-makers and field marshals of the world's activities.

Occasionally, through "leakages," one of the enigmatic men or women of earth will be found to have "dabbled" in the black arts. These, of course, are brought to light as the "mystery men" of history. Names like Rasputin, Zaharoff, Cagliostro, Rosenberg and their ilk are links—clues, so to speak, of the true legacy of Satan . . . a legacy which transcends ethnic, racial and economic differences and temporal ideologies, as well. The Satanist has always ruled the earth . . . and always will, by whatever name he is called.

One thing stands sure: the standards, philosophy and

practices set forth on these pages are those employed by the most self-realized and powerful humans on earth. In the secret thoughts of each man and woman, still motivated by sound and unclouded minds, resides the potential of the Satanist, as always has been. The sign of the horns shall appear to many, now, rather than the few; and the magician will stand forth that he may be recognized.

(EARTH)

THE BOOK OF BELIAL

THE MASTERY OF THE EARTH

The greatest appeal of magic is not in its application, but in its esoteric meanderings. The element of mystery which so heavily enshrouds the practice of the black arts has been fostered, deliberately or out of ignorance, by those who often claim the highest expertise in such matters. If the shortest distance between two points is a straight line, then established occultists would do well as maze-makers. The basic principles of ceremonial magic have been relegated for so long to infinitely classified bits of scholastic mysticism, that the would-be wizard becomes the *victim* of the very art of misdirection which *he, himself, should be employing!* An analogy may be drawn of the student of applied psychology who, though knowing all of the answers, cannot make friends.

What good is a study of falsehoods, unless everyone believes in falsehoods? Many, of course, DO believe in falsehoods, but still ACT according to natural law. It is upon this premise that Satanic magic is based. This is a primer—a basic text on materialistic magic. It is a Satanic *McGuffey's Reader.*

Belial means "without a master," and symbolizes true independence, self-sufficiency, and personal accomplishment. Belial represents the earth element, and herein will be found magic with both feet on the ground—real, hard-core, magical procedure—not mystical platitudes devoid of objective reason. Probe no longer. Here is bedrock!

THE THEORY AND PRACTICE
OF
SATANIC MAGIC

(Definition and Purpose)

THE definition of magic, as used in this book, is: "The change in situations or events in accordance with one's will, which would, using normally accepted methods, be unchangeable." This admittedly leaves a large area for personal interpretation. It will be said, by some, that these instructions and procedures are nothing more than applied psychology, or scientific fact, called by "magical" terminology—until they arrive at a passage in the text that is "based on no known scientific finding." It is for this reason that no attempt has been made to limit the explanations set forth to a set nomenclature. Magic is never totally scientifically explainable, but science has always been, at one time or another, considered magic.

There is no difference between "White" and "Black" magic, except in the smug hypocrisy, guilt-ridden righteousness, and self-deceit of the "White" magician himself. In the classical religious tradition, "White" magic is performed for altruistic, benevolent, and "good" purposes; while "Black" magic is used for self-aggrandizement, personal power, and "evil" purposes. No one on earth ever pursued occult studies, metaphysics, yoga, or any other "white light" concept, without ego gratification and personal power as a goal. It just so happens that some people enjoy wearing hair shirts, and others prefer velvet or silk. What is pleasure to one, is pain to another, and the same applies to "good" and "evil." Every practitioner of witchcraft is convinced that he or she is doing the "right" thing.

Magic falls into two categories, ritual or ceremonial, and non-ritual or manipulative. Ritual magic consists of the performance of a formal ceremony, taking place, at least in part, within the confines of an area set aside for such purposes and at a specific time. Its main function is to isolate the otherwise dissipated adrenal and other emotionally induced energy, and convert it into a dynamically transmittable force. It is purely an emotional, rather than intellectual, act. Any and all intellectual activity must take place *before* the ceremony, not during it. This type of magic is sometimes known as "GREATER MAGIC."

Non-ritual or manipulative magic, sometimes called "LESSER MAGIC," consists of the wile and guile obtained through various devices and contrived situations, which when utilized, can create "change, in accordance with one's will." In olden times this would be called "fascination," "glamour," or the "evil eye."

Most of the victims of the witch trials were not witches. Often the victims were eccentric old women who were either senile or did not conform to society. Others were exceptionally attractive women who turned the heads of the men in power, and were not responsive to their advances. The real witches were rarely executed, or even brought to trial, as they were proficient in the art of enchantment and could charm the men and save their own lives. Most of the real witches were sleeping with the inquisitors. This is the origin of the word "glamour." The antiquated meaning of glamour is witchcraft. The most important asset to the modern witch is her ability to be alluring, or to utilize glamour. The word "fascination" has a similarly occult origin. Fascination was the term applied to the evil eye. To fix a person's gaze, in other words, fascinate, was to curse them with the evil eye. Therefore, if a woman had the ability to fascinate men, she was regarded as a witch.

Learning to effectively utilize the command to LOOK, is an integral part of a witch's or warlock's training. To manipulate a person, you must first be able to attract and hold his attention.

The three methods by which the command to look can be accomplished are the utilization of sex, sentiment, or wonder, or any combination of these. A witch must, *honestly*, decide into which category she most naturally falls. The first category, that of sex, is self-evident. If a woman is attractive or sexually appealing, she should do everything in her power to make herself as enticing as possible, thereby using sex as her most powerful tool. Once she has gained the man's attention, by using her sex appeal, she is free to manipulate him to her will. The second category is sentiment. Usually older women fit into this category. This would include the "cookie lady" type witch, who might live in a little cottage, and be thought of by people as being a bit eccentric. Children are usually enchanted by the fantasy that this type of witch can provide for them, and young adults seek her out for her sage-like advice. Through their innocence, children can recognize her magical power. By conforming to an image of the sweet little old lady next door, she can employ the art of misdirection to accomplish her goals. The third category is the wonder theme. This category would apply to the woman who is strange or awesome in her appearance. By making her strange appearance work for her, she can manipulate people simply because they are fearful of the consequences should they not do as she asks.

Many women fit into more than one of these categories. For example, the young girl who has an appearance of freshness and innocence, but at the same time is very sexy, combines sex and sentiment. Or, the femme fatale who combines sex appeal with sinister overtones, uses sex and wonder. After evaluating her assets, each witch must decide into which category or combination of categories she fits, and then utilize these assets in their proper form.

To be a successful warlock, a man must similarly fit himself into the proper category. The handsome or sexually appealing man would, naturally, fit into the first category—sex. The second, or sentiment category would apply to the older man who has, perhaps, an elfin or forest wizard appearance. The sweet old grandpa (often a dirty old man!) would also be in the sentiment category. The third type would be the man who presents a sinister or diabolic appearance. Each of these men would apply his particular brand of the command to look, in much the same way as the women previously described.

Visual imagery utilized for emotional reaction is certainly the most important device incorporated in the practice of lesser magic. Anyone who is foolish enough to say "looks don't mean a thing" is indeed deluded. Good looks are unnecessary, but "looks" certainly are needed!

Odor is another important manipulative factor in lesser magic. Remember, animals fear and distrust anyone or anything that doesn't smell! And even though we may, as human animals, deny many of the judgments based on this sense consciously, we still are motivated by our sense of smell just as surely as any all-fours animal. If you are a man, and wish to enchant a woman, allow the natural secretions of your body to pervade the atmosphere immediately around you, and work in animalistic contrast to the vestments of social politeness that you wear upon your back. If you, as a woman, wish to bewitch a man, do not fear that you might "offend" simply because the oils and fragrances of your flesh have not been scrubbed away, or that place between your thighs is not dry and sterile. These natural odors are the sexual stimulants which nature, in her magical wisdom, has provided.

The sentiment stimulants are those odors that will appeal to pleasant memories and nostalgia. The enchanting of a man, through his stomach, is first established by the smell of cooking! A "sentiment" type of witch will find this one of the most useful of all charms. It is not so facetious to dwell upon the technique of the man who wished to charm the young lady who had been displaced from her home of childhood joys, which happened to be a fishing village. Wise to the ways of lesser magic, he neatly tucked a mackerel into his trousers pocket, and reaped the rewards that great fondness may often bring.

THE THREE TYPES
OF
SATANIC RITUAL

HERE are three types of ceremony incorporated in the practice of Satanic magic. Each of these correspond to a basic human emotion. The first of these we shall call a sex ritual.

A sex ritual is what is commonly known as a love charm or spell. The purpose in performing such a ritual is to create desire on the part of the person whom you desire, or to summon a sex partner to fulfill your desires. If you have no specific person or type of person in mind strong enough to cause direct sexual feeling culminating in orgasm, you will not succeed in performing a successful working. The reason for this is that even if the ritual was successful, by accident, what good would it serve if you could not take advantage of your eventual opportunity because of lack of stimulation or desire? It is easy to confuse enchantment for your ulterior motives, with spell-casting to satisfy your sexual desires.

Enchantment for self-aggrandizement, when accompanied by ceremonial magic, falls into the category of either the compassion or the destruction ritual, or possibly both. If you want or need something so badly you are sad or feel much anguish without it, and can obtain it through the use of glamour and enchantment, without causing hurt on another's part, then this would incorporate a compassion ritual to increase your power. If you wish to enchant or entrap a deserving victim for your own purposes, you would employ a destruction ritual. These formulas are to be adhered to, as applying the wrong type of ritual towards a desired result can lead to trouble of a complicated nature.

A good example of this is the girl who finds herself plagued by a relentless suitor. If she has done little to encourage him, then she should recognize him for the psychic vampire he is, and let him play his masochistic role. If, however, she has enchanted him frivolously, giving him every encouragement and then finds herself a steady object of sexual desire, much to her dismay, she has no one to blame but herself. Such exercises are only ego boosts, borne of an indoctrination of ego denial which makes these little bewitchments necessary. The Satanist has enough ego strength to use enchantments for her own sexual gratification, or to gain power or success of a specific nature.

The second type of ritual is of a compassionate nature. The compassion, or sentiment, ritual is performed for the purpose of helping others, or helping oneself. Health, domestic happiness, business activities, material success, and scholastic prowess are but a few of the situations covered in a compassion ritual. It might be said that this form of ceremony could fall into the realm of *genuine* charity, bearing in mind that "charity begins at home."

The third motivating force is that of destruction. This is a ceremony used for anger, annoyance, disdain, contempt, or just plain hate. It is known as a hex, curse, or destroying agent.

One of the greatest of all fallacies about the practice of ritual magic is the notion that one must believe in the powers of magic before one can be harmed or destroyed by them. Nothing could be farther from the truth, as the most receptive victims of curses have always been the greatest scoffers. The reason is frighteningly simple. The uncivilized tribesman is the first to run to his nearest witch-doctor or shaman when he feels a curse has been placed upon him by an enemy. The threat and presence of harm is with him consciously, and belief in the power of the curse is so strong that he will take every precaution against it. Thus, through the application of sympathetic magic, he will counteract any harm that might come his way. This man is watching his step, and not taking any chances.

On the other hand, the "enlightened" man, who doesn't place any stock in such "superstition," relegates his instinctive fear of the curse to his unconscious, thereby nourishing it into a phenomenally destructive force that will multiply with each succeeding misfortune. Of course, every time a new setback occurs, the non-believer will automatically deny any connection with the curse, *especially* to himself. This emphatic conscious denial of the potential of the curse is the very ingredient that will create its success, through setting-up of accident prone situations. In many instances, the victim will deny any magical significance to his fate, even unto his dying gasp—although the magician is perfectly satisfied, so long as his desired results occur. It must be remembered that *it matters not whether anyone attaches any significance to your working, so long as the results of the working are in accordance with your will.* The super-logician will always explain the connection of the magical ritual to the end result as "coincidence."

Whether magic is performed for constructive or destructive purposes, the success of the operation is dependent on the receptivity of the person who is to receive the blessing or curse, as the case may be. In the case of a sex or compassion ritual, it *helps* if the recipient has faith and believes in magic, but the victim of a hex or curse is much more prone to destruction if he DOES NOT believe in it! So long as man knows the meaning of fear, he will need the ways and means to defend himself against his fears. No one knows everything, and as long as there is wonder, there will always be an apprehension of the unknown, where there are potentially dangerous forces. It is this natural fear of the unknown, a first cousin to the fascination *towards* the unknown, that impels the man of logic towards his very explanations. Obviously, the man of science is motivated to discovery by his very sense of wonder. And yet, how sad that this man who calls himself logical is often the last to recognize the essence of ritual magic.

If religious faith and fervor can make bleeding wounds

appear on the body in approximation to the wounds supposedly inflicted on Christ, it is called stigmata. These wounds appear as a result of compassion driven to an emotionally violent extreme. Why, then, should there be any doubt as to the destructive extremes of fear and terror. The so-called demons have the power to destroy in a flesh rending manner, theoretically, as much as a handful of nails, long rusted away, can create blood-dripping ecstasy in a person convinced he is hooked upon the cross of Calvary.

Therefore, never attempt to convince the skeptic upon whom you wish to place a curse. Allow him to scoff. To enlighten him would lessen your chance of success. Listen with benign assurance as he laughs at your magic, knowing his days are filled with turmoil all the while. If he is despicable enough, by Satan's grace, he might even die—laughing!

A WORD OF WARNING!

TO THOSE WHO WOULD PRACTICE THESE ARTS—

Concerning Sex or Lust: *Take full advantage of spells and charms that work; if you be a man, plunge your erect member into her with lascivious delight; if you be a woman, open wide your loins in lewd anticipation.*

Concerning Compassion: *Be resolved that you'll have no regrets at the expense of the help that you have given others, should their new-found blessings place an obstacle in your path. Be grateful for things that come to you through the use of magic.*

Concerning Destruction: *Be certain you* DO NOT *care if the intended victim lives or dies, before you throw your curse, and having caused their destruction, revel, rather than feel remorse.*

HEED WELL THESE RULES—OR IN EACH CASE YOU WILL SEE A REVERSAL OF YOUR DESIRES WHICH WILL HARM, RATHER THAN HELP, YOU!

THE RITUAL, OR
"INTELLECTUAL DECOMPRESSION,"
CHAMBER

A MAGICAL ceremony may be performed by oneself or in a group, but the advantages of each should be made clear.

A group ritual is certainly much more of a reinforcement of faith, and an instillation of power, than is a private ceremony. The massing together of persons who are dedicated to a common philosophy is bound to insure a renewal of confidence in the power of magic. The pageantry of religion is what has sustained it. When religion consistently becomes a solitary situation it reaches into that realm of self-denial which runs concurrent with anti-social behavior.

It is for this reason that the Satanist should attempt to seek out others with whom to engage in these ceremonies.

In the case of a curse or destruction ritual, it sometimes helps the magician if his desires are intensified by other members of the group. There is nothing in this type of ceremony which would lead to embarrassment on the part of those conducting a ritual of this sort, since anger and the symbolic destruction of the intended victim are the essential ingredients.

On the other hand, a compassion ritual, with its unashamed shedding of tears, or a sex ritual, with its masturbatory and orgasmic overtones, would most likely succeed best if privately performed.

There is no place for self-consciousness in the ritual chamber, unless that very self-consciousness is an integral part of the role being played, and can be used to good advantage—i.e.: the shame felt by a prudent woman serving as an altar, who, through her embarrassment, feels sexual stimulation.

Even in a totally personalized ritual, however, the standardized preliminary invocations and devices should be employed before the intimate fantasies and acting out occur. The formal part of the ritual can be performed in the same room or chamber as the personalized working—or, the formal ceremony in one place, the personal in another. The beginning and end of the ritual must be conducted within the confines of the ritual chamber containing the symbolic devices (altar, chalice, etc.).

The formalized beginning and end of the ceremony acts as a dogmatic, anti-intellectual device, the purpose of which is to disassociate the activities and frame of reference of the outside world from that of the ritual chamber, where the whole will must be employed. This facet of the ceremony is *most* important to the intellectual, as he *especially* requires the "decompression chamber" effect of the chants, bells, candles, and other trappings, before he can put his pure and willful desires to work for himself, in the projection and utilization of his imagery.

The "intellectual decompression chamber" of the Satanic temple might be considered a training school for temporary ignorance, as are ALL religious services! The difference is that the Satanist KNOWS he is practicing a form of contrived ignorance in order to expand his will, whereas another religionist doesn't—or if he does know, he practices that form of self-deceit which forbids such recognition. His ego is already too shaky from his religious inculcation to allow himself to admit to such a thing as self-imposed ignorance!

THE INGREDIENTS USED IN THE PERFORMANCE OF SATANIC MAGIC

A. Desire

THE first ingredient in the performance of a ritual is desire, otherwise known as motivation, temptation, or emotional persuasion. If you do not truly desire any end result, you should not attempt to perform a working.

There is no such thing as a "practice" working, and the only way that a magician could do "tricks" such as moving inanimate objects, would be to have a strong emotional need to do so. It is true that if the magician wishes to gain power through impressing others with his feats of magic, he must produce tangible proof of his ability. The Satanic concept of magic, however, fails to find gratification in the proving of magical prowess.

The Satanist performs his ritual to insure the outcome of his desires, and he would not waste his time nor force of will on something so inconclusive as rolling a pencil off a table, etc. through the application of magic. The amount of energy needed to levitate a teacup (genuinely) would be of sufficient force to place an idea in a group of people's heads half-way across the earth, in turn, motivating them in accordance with your will. The Satanist knows that even if you succeeded in lifting the teacup from the table, it would be assumed that trickery was used anyway. Therefore, if the Satanist wants to float objects in mid-air, he uses wires, mirrors, or other devices, and saves his force for self-aggrandizement. All "gifted" mediums and white-light mystics practice pure and applied stage magic, with their blindfolds and sealed envelopes, and any fairly competent stage magician, carnival worker, or lodge-hall entertainer can duplicate the same effect—although lacking, perhaps, the sanctimonious "spiritual" overtones.

A little child learns that if he wishes for something hard enough, it will come true. This is meaningful. Wishing indicates desire, whereas prayer is accompanied by apprehension. Scripture has twisted desire into lust, covetousness, and greed. Be as a child, and do not stifle desire, lest you lose touch with the first ingredient in the performance of magic. Be led into temptation, and take that which tempts, whenever you can!

B. Timing

In every successful situation, one of the most important ingredients is the proper timing. In the performance of a magical ritual, timing can mean success or failure to an even greater extent. The best time to cast your spell or charm, hex or curse, is when your target is at his most receptive state. Receptivity to the will of the magician is assured when the recipient is as passive as possible. No matter how strong-willed one is, he is naturally passive while he is asleep; therefore, the best time to throw your magical energy towards your target is when he or she sleeps.

There are certain periods of the sleep cycle that are better than others for susceptibility to outside influences. When a person is normally fatigued from a day's activities, he will "sleep like a log" until his mind and body are rested. This period of profound sleep usually lasts about four to six hours, after which the period of "dream sleep" occurs which lasts two or three hours, or until awakening. It is during this "dream sleep" that the mind is most receptive to outside or unconscious influence.

Let us assume the magician wishes to cast a spell on a person who would usually retire at 11 o'clock in the evening, and rise at 7 o'clock in the morning. The most effective time to perform a ritual would be about 5 o'clock in the morning, or two hours before the recipient awakens.

It is to be emphasized that the magician must be at his peak of efficiency, as he represents the "sending" factor when he performs his ritual. Traditionally speaking, witches and sorcerers are night people, and understandably so. What better schedule on which to live, for the sending of thoughts towards unsuspecting sleepers! If only people were aware of the thoughts injected into their minds while they slept! The dream state is the birthplace of much of the future. Great thoughts are manifest upon awakening, and the mind that retains, in conscious form, these thoughts, shall produce much. But he who is guided by thoughts unrecognized is led into situations that will later be interpreted as "fate," "God's will," or accident.

There are other times in each person's day that lend themselves to the receiving of the will of the wizard. Those times when day-dreaming or boredom ensue, or when time hangs heavy, are fertile periods of suggestibility.

If a woman is the target for your spell, do not forget the importance of the menstrual cycle. If man were not dulled through his stifling evolutionary development, he would know, as an all-fours animal knows, when the female was most sexually inclined. Man's snout, however unsullied by cheap opiates, is not normally equipped to ferret out such tell-tale erotic scents. Even if he were so endowed with such olfactory powers, the object of his quest would most likely "throw him off the scent" through the use of massive doses of perfumery to cover and smother the "offending" effluvium, or eliminate detection completely, by the astringent action of powerful deodorants.

Despite these discouraging factors, man is still motivated to desire or be repelled, as the case may be, by his unconscious recognition of the change in woman's body chemistry. This is accomplished in the form of a sensory cue, which is olfactory in its nature. To go backwards, in what would amount to a return to the all-fours animal, would seem to be the best exercise for the conscious application of these powers, but to the squeamish might smack of lycanthropy. There is, however, an easier way, and that is to simply ascertain the dates and frequency of the menstrual cycle of the woman who is your target. It is immediately before and after the period itself that the average woman is most sexually approachable. Therefore, the magician will find the sleep period during these times most effective for the instillation of thoughts or motivations of a sexual nature.

Witches and sorceresses have a much greater range of time in which to cast their spells toward the men of their choice. Because man is more consistent in his sexual drives than woman (although there are many women with equal or even greater lusts), day to day timing is not as important. Any man who is not already drained of all sexual energy is a "sitting duck" for the proficient witch. The time of the year following the spring equinox is the most fraught with sexual vigor in a man, and he asserts himself accordingly; but the witch, in turn, must work her magic stronger, as she will find his eyes will stray.

Should the fearful ask, "Is there no defense against such witchery?" it must be answered thus—"Yes, there is protection. You must never sleep, never daydream, never be without a vital thought, and never have an open mind. Then you shall be protected from the forces of magic."

C. Imagery

The adolescent boy who takes great care in carving, on a tree, a heart containing his and his love object's initials; the little chap who sits by the hour drawing his conception of sleek automobiles; the tiny girl who rocks a scuffed and ragged doll in her arms, and thinks of it as her beautiful little baby—these capable witches and warlocks, these natural magicians, are employing the magical ingredient known as imagery, and the success of any ritual depends on it.

Children, not knowing nor caring if they possess artistic skill or other creative talents, pursue their goals through the use of imagery of their own manufacture, whereas "civilized" adults are much more critical of their own creative efforts. This is why a "primitive" magician can utilize a mud doll or crude drawing to successful advantage in his magical ceremonies. To HIM, the image is as accurate as needs be.

Anything which serves to intensify the emotions during a ritual will contribute to its success. Any drawing, painting, sculpture, writing, photograph, article of clothing, scent, sound, music, tableau, or contrived situation that can be incorporated into the ceremony will serve the sorcerer well.

Imagery is a constant reminder, an intellect-saving device, a working substitute for the real thing. Imagery can be manipulated, set up, modified, and created, all according to the will of the magician, and the very blueprint that is created by imagery becomes the formula which leads to reality.

If you wish to enjoy sexual pleasures with the one of your choice, you must create the situation you desire on paper, canvas, by the written word, etc., in as overstated a way as possible, as an integral part of the ceremony.

If you have material desires, you must gaze upon images of them—surround yourself with the smells and sounds conducive to them—create a lodestone which will attract the situation or thing that you wish!

To insure the destruction of an enemy, you must destroy them by proxy! They must be shot, stabbed, sickened, burned, smashed, drowned, or rent in the most vividly convincing manner! It is easy to see why the religions of the right-hand path frown upon the creation of "graven images." The imagery used by the sorcerer is a working mechanism for material reality, which is totally opposed to esoteric spirituality.

A Greek gentleman of magical persuasion once wanted a woman who would satisfy his every desire, and so obsessed with the unfound object of his dreams was he, that he went about constructing such a wonderful creature. His work completed, he fell so convincingly and irrevocably in love with the woman he had created that she was no longer stone, but mortal

125

flesh, and alive and warm; and so the magus, Pygmalion, received the greatest of magical benedictions, and the beautiful Galatea was his.

D. Direction

One of the most overlooked ingredients in the working of magic is the accumulation and subsequent direction of force toward an effective end.

Altogether too many would-be witches and warlocks will perform a ritual, and then go about with tremendous anxiety waiting for the first sign of a successful working. For all intent and purpose, they might as well get down on their knees and pray, for their very anxiety in waiting for the desired results only nullifies any real chance of success. Furthermore, with this attitude, it is doubtful that enough concentrated energy to even perform a proper ceremony could be stored up in the first place.

To dwell upon or constantly complain about the situation upon which your ritual would be based only guarantees the weakening of what should be ritualistically directed force, by spreading it thin and diluting it. Once the desire has been established strongly enough to employ the forces of magic, then every attempt must be made to symbolically give vent to these wishes IN THE PERFORMANCE OF THE RITUAL—NOT before or after!

The purpose of the ritual is to FREE the magician from thoughts that would consume him, were he to dwell upon them constantly. Contemplation, daydreaming, and constant scheming burns up emotional energy that could be gathered together in a dynamically usable force; not to mention the fact that normal productivity is severely depleted by such consuming anxiety.

The witch who casts her spells between long waits by the telephone, anticipating her would-be lover's call; the destitute warlock who invokes Satan's blessing, then waits on pins and needles for the check to arrive; the man, saddened by the injustices wrought upon him, who, having cursed his enemy, plods his way, long of face, and furrowed of brow—all are common examples of misdirected emotional energy.

Small wonder that the "white" magician fears retribution after casting an "evil" spell! Retribution, to the guilt-ridden sender, would be assured, by their very conscience-stricken state!

E. The Balance Factor

The Balance Factor is an ingredient employed in the practice of ritual magic which applies to the casting of lust and compassion rituals more than in the throwing of a curse. This ingredient is a small, but extremely important one.

A complete knowledge and awareness of this factor is an ability few witches and warlocks ever attain. This is, simply, knowing the proper type of individual and situation to work your magic on for the easiest and best results. Knowing one's own limitations is a rather odd bit of introspection, it would seem, for a person who should be able to perform the impossible; but under many conditions it can make the difference between success and failure.

If, in attempting to attain your goal through either greater or lesser magic, you find yourself failing consistently, think about these things: Have you been the victim of a misdirected, over-blown ego which has caused you to want something or someone when the chances are virtually non-existent? Are you a talentless, tone-deaf individual who is attempting, through magic, to receive great acclaim for your unmusical voice? Are you a plain, glamorless witch with oversized feet, nose, and ego, combined with an advanced case of acne, who is casting love spells to catch a handsome young movie star? Are you a gross, lumpy, lewd-mouthed, snaggle-toothed loafer who is desirous of a luscious young stripper? If so, you'd better learn to use the balance factor, or else expect to fail consistently!

To be able to adjust one's wants to one's capabilities is a great talent, and too many people fail to realize that if they are unable to attain the maximum, "a half a loaf *can* be better than none." The chronic loser is always the man who, having nothing, if unable to make a million dollars, will reject any chance to make fifty thousand with a disgruntled sneer.

One of the magician's greatest weapons is knowing himself; his talents, abilities, physical attractions and detractions, etc., and when, where, and *with whom* to utilize them! The man with nothing to offer, who approaches the man who is successful with grandiose advice and promise of great wealth, has the alacrity of the flea climbing up the elephant's leg with the intention of rape!

The aspiring witch who deludes herself into thinking that a powerful enough working will *always* succeed, despite a magical imbalance, is forgetting one essential rule: MAGIC IS LIKE NATURE ITSELF, AND SUCCESS IN MAGIC REQUIRES WORKING IN HARMONY WITH NATURE, NOT AGAINST IT.

THE
SATANIC RITUAL

A. NOTES WHICH ARE TO BE OBSERVED BEFORE BEGINNING RITUAL:

1 Person performing ritual stands facing the altar and symbol of Baphomet throughout ritual, except when other positions are specifically indicated.

2 If possible, altar should be against west wall.

3 In rituals performed by one person the role of priest is not required. When more than one person is involved in the ceremony, one of them must act as priest. In a private ritual the sole performer follows the instructions for the priest.

4 Whenever the words "Shemhamforash!" and "Hail Satan!" are spoken by the person acting as priest, the other participants will repeat the words after him. The gong is struck following the other participants' response to "Hail Satan!"

5 Conversing (except within the context of the ceremony) and smoking are prohibited after the bell is rung at the beginning, until after it is again rung at the end of the ritual.

6 The Book of Belial contains the principles of Satanic magic and ritual. *Before* attempting the rituals in the *Book of Leviathan*, it is imperative that you read *and understand the complete Book of Belial*. Until you have done so, no degree of success can be expected from the thirteen steps which follow.

B. THE THIRTEEN STEPS

(See *Devices Used in a Satanic Ritual* on pages 134-140
for detailed instructions)

1   Dress for ritual.

2   Assemble devices for ritual; light candles and shut out
    all outside light sources; place parchments to right and
    left of the altar as indicated.

3   If a woman is used as the altar she now takes her posi-
    tion—head pointing south, feet pointing north.

4   Purification of the air by ringing of the bell.

5   "Invocation to Satan" and "Infernal Names" which
    follow (see *Book of Leviathan*) are now read aloud by
    priest. Participants will repeat each Infernal Name after
    it has been said by priest.

6   Drink from chalice.

7   Turning counter-clockwise, the priest points with the
    sword to each cardinal point of the compass and calls
    forth the respective Princes of Hell: Satan from the
    south, Lucifer from the east, Belial from the north, and
    Leviathan from the west.

8   Perform benediction with the phallus (if one is used).

9   Priest reads aloud appropriate invocation for respective
    ceremony: Lust, Compassion, or Destruction (see *Book
    of Leviathan*).

10 In the case of a personalized ritual this step is extremely
    important. Solitude is compatible with the expressing
    of the most secret desires, and no attempt to "hold
    back" should be made in the acting out, verbalizing, or
    casting of images pertaining to your desires. It is at this
    step that your "blueprint" is drawn, wrapped, and sent
    off to the recipient of your working.

(A)

To Summon One For Lustful Purpose Or Establish A Sexually Gratifying Situation

Leave the area of the altar and remove yourself to that place, either in the same room or without, that will be most conducive to the working of the respective ritual. Then, fashion whatever imagery you possibly can that will parallel in as exact a way possible the situation towards which you strive. Remember, you have five senses to utilize, so do not feel you must limit your imagery to one. Here are devices that may be employed (either alone, or in any combination):

a   graphic imagery such as drawings, paintings, etc.

b   written imagery such as stories, plays, descriptions of desires and eventual outcome of same.

c   acting out the desire in tableau or playlet, either as yourself or portraying the role of the object of your desire (transference), using any devices necessary to intensify imagery.

d   any odors relative to the desired person or situation.

e   any sounds or background noises conducive to a strong image.

Intense sexual feeling should accompany this step of the ritual, and after sufficient imagery is obtained, as strong an orgasm as is possible should serve as climax to this step. This climax should be attained using any masturbatory or auto-erotic means necessary. After orgasm is obtained, return to the location of the altar and proceed with step #11, page 134.

(B)

To Insure Help Or Success For One Who Has Your Sympathy Or Compassion (Including Yourself)

Remain in close proximity of the altar and with as vivid a mental image as possible of the person you wish to help (or intense self-pity), state your desire in your own terms. Should your emotions be genuine enough, they will be accompanied by the shedding of tears, which should be allowed to flow without restraint. After this exercise in sentiment is completed, proceed to step #11, page 134.

(C)

To Cause The Destruction Of An Enemy

Remain in the area of the altar unless imagery is more easily obtained in another spot, such as in the vicinity of the victim. Producing the image of the victim, proceed to inflict the destruction upon the effigy in the manner of your choice. This can be done in the following ways:

  a   the sticking of pins or nails into a doll representing your victim; the doll may be cloth, wax, wood, vegetable matter, etc.
  b   the creation of graphic imagery depicting the method of your victim's destruction; drawings, paintings, etc.
  c   the creation of a vivid literary description of your victim's ultimate end.
  d   a detailed soliloquy directed at the intended victim, describing his torments and annihilation.

     e   mutilation, injury, infliction of pain or illness by proxy using any other means or devices desired.

Intense, calculated hatred and disdain should accompany this step of the ceremony, and no attempt should be made to stop this step until the expended energy results in a state of relative exhaustion on the part of the magician. When this exhaustion ensues, proceed to step #11.

11(a)   If requests are written, they are now read aloud by the priest and then burned in the flames of the appropriate candle. "Shemhamforash!" and "Hail Satan!" is said after each request.

11(b)   If requests are given verbally, participants (one at a time) now tell them to the priest. He then repeats in his own words (those which are most emotionally stimulating to him) the request. "Shemhamforash!" and "Hail Satan!" is said after each request.

12   Appropriate Enochian Key is now read by the priest, as evidence of the participants' allegiance to the Powers of Darkness.

13   Ringing of the bell as pollutionary, and then the words "SO IT IS DONE" are spoken by the priest.

END OF RITUAL

C. DEVICES USED IN A SATANIC RITUAL

CLOTHING

Black robes are worn by the male participants. The robes may be cowled or hooded, and if desired may cover the face. The purpose in covering the face is to allow the participant freedom to express emotion in the face, without concern. It also lessens distraction on the part of one participant towards another. Female participants wear garments which are sexually suggestive; or all black clothing for older women. Amulets bearing the sigil of Baphomet or the traditional pentagram of Satan are worn by all participants.

Robes are donned by men before entering the ritual chamber, and are worn throughout the ritual. Men may substitute all black clothing for black robes.

Black is chosen for the attire in the ritual chamber because it is symbolic of the Powers of Darkness. Sexually appealing clothing is worn by women for the purpose of stimulating the emotions of the male participants, and thereby intensifying the outpouring of adrenal or bio-electrical energy which will insure a more powerful working.

ALTAR

Man's earliest altars were living flesh and blood; and man's natural instincts and predilections were the foundation on which his religions were based. Later religions, in making man's natural inclinations sinful, perverted his living altars into slabs of stone and lumps of metal.

Satanism is a religion of the flesh, rather than of the spirit; therefore, an altar of flesh is used in Satanic ceremonies. The purpose of an altar is to serve as a focal point towards which all attention is focused during a ceremony. A nude woman is used as the altar in Satanic rituals because woman is the natural passive receptor, and represents the earth mother.

In some rituals nudity for the woman serving as altar may be impractical, so she may be clothed or partially covered. If a female is performing the ritual alone, no woman need be used for the altar. If no female is used for the altar, the elevated plane used for her to lie upon may be used to hold other devices for the ritual. For large group rituals a trapezoidal altar about 3 to 4 feet high and 5½ to 6 feet long can be specially constructed for the woman to lie upon. If this is impractical, or in private ceremonies, any elevated plane may be used. If a woman is used for the altar, the other devices may be placed upon a table within easy reach of the priest.

SYMBOL OF BAPHOMET

The symbol of Baphomet was used by the Knights Templar to represent Satan. Through the ages this symbol has been called by many different names. Among these are: The Goat of Mendes, The Goat of a Thousand Young, The Black Goat, The Júdas Goat, and perhaps most appropriately, The Scapegoat.

Baphomet represents the Powers of Darkness combined with the generative fertility of the goat. In its "pure" form the pentagram is shown encompassing the figure of a man in the five points of the star—three points up, two pointing down—symbolizing man's spiritual nature. In Satanism the pentagram is also used, but since Satanism represents the carnal instincts of man, or the opposite of the spiritual nature, the pentagram is inverted to perfectly accommodate the head of the goat—its horns, representing duality, thrust upwards in defiance; the other three points inverted, or the trinity denied. The Hebraic figures around the outer circle of the symbol which stem from the magical teachings of the Kabala, spell out "Leviathan," the serpent of the watery abyss, and identified with Satan. These figures correspond to the five points of the inverted star.

The symbol of Baphomet is placed on the wall above the altar.

CANDLES

The candles used in Satanic ritual represent the light of Lucifer—the bearer of light, enlightenment, the living flame, burning desire, and the Flames of the Pit.

Only black and white candles are to be used in Satanic ritual. Never use more than one white candle; but as many black candles as are required to illuminate the ritual chamber may be used. At least one black candle is placed to the left of the altar, representing the Powers of Darkness and the left-hand path. Other black candles are placed where needed for illumination. One white candle is placed to the right of the altar, representing the hypocrisy of white light "magicians" and the followers of the right-hand path. No other light source is to be used.

Black candles are used for power and success for the participants of the ritual, and are used to consume the parchments on which blessings requested by the ritual participants are written. The white candle is used for destruction of enemies. Parchments upon which curses are written are burned in the flame of the white candle.

BELL

The shattering effect of the bell is used to mark both the beginning and the end of the ritual. The priest rings the bell nine times, turning counter clockwise and directing the tolling towards the four cardinal points of the compass. This is done once at the beginning of the ritual to clear and purify the air of all external sounds, and once again at the end of the ritual to intensify the working and act as a pollutionary indicating finality.

The tonal quality of the bell used should be loud and penetrating, rather than soft and tinkling.

CHALICE

In Satanic ritual the chalice or goblet used represents the Chalice of Ecstasy. Ideally, the chalice should be made of silver, but if a silver chalice can not be obtained, one made from another metal, glass, or crockery may be used—*anything but gold*. Gold has always been associated with white-light religions and the Heavenly Realm.

The chalice is to be drunk from first by the priest, then by one assistant. In private rituals the person performing the ceremony drains the chalice.

ELIXIR

The stimulating fluid or Elixir of Life used by the Pagans has been corrupted into sacramental wine by the Christian faith. Originally, the liquor used in Pagan rituals was drunk to relax and intensify the emotions of those involved in the ceremony. Satanism does not sacrifice its god, as do other religions. The Satanist practices no such form of symbolic cannibalism, and returns the sacramental wine used by the Christians to its original purpose—that of stimulating the emotions necessary to Satanic ritual. Wine itself need not be used—whatever drink is most stimulating and pleasing to the palate is in order.

The Elixir of Life is to be drunk from the Chalice of Ecstasy, as indicated above, immediately following the Invocation to Satan.

SWORD

The Sword of Power is symbolic of aggressive force, and acts as an extension and intensifier of the arm with which the priest uses to gesture and point. A parallel to this is the pointing stick or blasting wand used in other forms of magical ritual.

The sword is held by the priest and is used to point towards the symbol of Baphomet during the Invocation to Satan. It is also used, as indicated in *Steps of Ritual*, when calling forth the four Princes of Hell. The priest thrusts the point of the sword through the parchment containing the message or request after it has been read aloud; it is then used to hold the parchment while introduced into the candle flame. While hearing the requests of other participants, and while repeating same, the priest places the sword atop their heads (in traditional "knighting" fashion).

For private rituals, if a sword cannot be obtained, a long knife, cane, or similar staff may be used.

PHALLUS

The phallus is a Pagan fertility symbol which represents generation, virility, and aggression. This is yet another device which has been blasphemously converted to fit the guilt-ridden ceremonies of Christianity. The phallus is a non-hypocritical version of the aspergillim, or "holy water sprinkler" used in Catholicism—quite a metamorphosis of the common penis!

The phallus is held in both hands of one of the priest's assistants, and methodically shaken twice towards each cardinal point of the compass, for the benediction of the house.

Any phallic symbol may be used. If none is obtainable one may be made from plaster, wood, clay, wax, etc. The phallus is necessary only in organized group rituals.

GONG

The gong is used to call upon the forces of Darkness. It is to be struck once after the participants have repeated the priest's words, "Hail Satan." A gong is necessary only in organized group rituals. For the best tonal quality a concert gong is preferred, but if one cannot be obtained any gong with a full, rich tone may be used.

PARCHMENT

Parchment is used because its organic properties are compatible with the elements of nature. In keeping with the Satanic views on sacrifice, the parchment used would be made from the skin of a sheep which was, by necessity, killed for food. An animal is *never* slaughtered for the purpose of using all or a part of that animal in a Satanic ritual. If commercial parchment which has been made from already slaughtered sheep cannot be obtained, plain paper may be substituted.

The parchment is the means by which the written message

or request can be consumed by the candle flame and sent out into the ether. The request is written on parchment or paper, read aloud by the priest, and then burned in the flame of either the black or white candle—whichever is appropriate for the particular request. Before the ritual begins curses are placed to the right of the priest, and charms or blessings are placed to the left of him.

(WATER)

THE BOOK OF LEVIATHAN

THE RAGING SEA

Despite all non-verbalists' protests to the contrary, soaring heights of emotional ecstasy or raging pangs of anguish can be attained through verbal communication. If the magical ceremony is to employ all sensory awarenesses, then the proper sounds must be invoked. It is certainly true that "actions speak louder than words," but words become as monuments to thoughts.

Perhaps the most noticeable shortcoming in the printed magical conjurations of the past is the lack of emotion developed upon the reciting of them. An old wizard known to the author, who was once employing a self-composed invocation of great personal meaning in the light of his magical desires, ran out of words just as his ritual was moments short of its successful culmination. Aware of the necessity of keeping his emotional response generating, he quickly adlibbed the first emotion-provoking words that came to mind—a few stanzas of a poem by Rudyard Kipling! Thus, with this final burst of glory-charged adrenalin, was he able to finalize an effective working!

The invocations which follow are designed to serve as proclamations of certainty, not whining apprehension. For this reason they are devoid of shallow offerings-up and hollow charities. Leviathan, the great Dragon from the Watery Abyss, roars forth as the surging sea, and these invocations are his tribunals.

INVOCATION
TO
SATAN

In nomine Dei nostri Satanas Luciferi excelsi!

In the name of Satan, the Ruler of the earth, the King of the world, I command the forces of Darkness to bestow their Infernal power upon me!

Open wide the gates of Hell and come forth from the abyss to greet me as your brother (sister) and friend!

Grant me the indulgences of which I speak!

I have taken thy name as a part of myself! I live as the beasts of the field, rejoicing in the fleshly life! I favor the just and curse the rotten!

By all the Gods of the Pit, I command that these things of which I speak shall come to pass!

Come forth and answer to your names by manifesting my desires!

OH HEAR THE NAMES:

THE INFERNAL NAMES*

Abaddon	Chemosh	Loki
Adramelech	Cimeries	Mammon
Ahpuch	Coyote	Mania
Ahriman	Dagon	Mantus
Amon	Damballa	Marduk
Apollyn	Demogorgon	Mastema
Asmodeus	Diabolus	Melek Taus
Astaroth	Dracula	Mephistopheles
Azazel	Emma-O	Metztli
Baalberith	Euronymous	Mictian
Balaam	Fenriz	Midgard
Baphomet	Gorgo	Milcom
Bast	Haborym	Moloch
Beelzebub	Hecate	Mormo
Behemoth	Ishtar	Naamah
Beherit	Kali	Nergal
Bilé	Lilith	Nihasa

---

* The Infernal names are listed here in alphabetical order purely to simplify referral to them.

When calling the names, all of them may be recited, or a given number of those most significant to the respective working may be chosen.

Whether all or only some of the names are called, they must be taken out of the rigidly organized form in which they are listed here and arranged in a phonetically effective roster.

Nija	Samnu	Tchort
O-Yama	Sedit	Tezcatlipoca
Pan	Sekhmet	Thamuz
Pluto	Set	Thoth
Proserpine	Shaitan	Tunrida
Pwcca	Shamad	Typhon
Rimmon	Shiva	Yaotzin
Sabazios	Supay	Yen-lo-Wang
Sammael	T'an-mo	

INVOCATION EMPLOYED TOWARDS
THE CONJURATION OF LUST

COME forth, Oh great spawn of the abyss and make thy presence manifest. I have set my thoughts upon the blazing pinnacle which glows with the chosen lust of the moments of increase and grows fervent in the turgid swell.

Send forth that messenger of voluptuous delights, and let these obscene vistas of my dark desires take form in future deeds and doings.

From the sixth tower of Satan there shall come a sign which joineth with those saltes within, and as such will move the body of the flesh of my summoning.

I have gathered forth my symbols and prepare my garnishings of the is to be, and the image of my creation lurketh as a seething basilisk awaiting his release.

The vision shall become as reality and through the nourishment that my sacrifice giveth, the angles of the first dimension shall become the substance of the third.

Go out into the void of night (light of day) and pierce that mind that respondeth with thoughts which leadeth to paths of lewd abandon.

(Male) My rod is athrust! The penetrating force of my venom shall shatter the sanctity of that mind which is barren of lust; and as the seed falleth, so shall its vapours be spread within that reeling brain benumbing it to helplessness according to my will! In the name of the great god Pan, may my secret thoughts be marshalled into the movements of the flesh of that which I desire!

Shemhamforash!   Hail Satan!

(Female)

My loins are aflame! The dripping of the nectar from my eager cleft shall act as pollen to that slumbering brain, and the mind that feels not lust shall on a sudden reel with crazed impulse. And when my mighty surge is spent, new wanderings shall begin; and that flesh which I desire shall come to me. In the names of the great harlot of Babylon, and of Lilith, and of Hecate, may my lust be fulfilled!

Shemhamforash!   Hail Satan!

INVOCATION EMPLOYED TOWARDS
THE CONJURATION OF DESTRUCTION

BEHOLD! The mighty voices of my vengeance smash the stillness of the air and stand as monoliths of wrath upon a plain of writhing serpents. I am become as a monstrous machine of annihilation to the festering fragments of the body of he (she) who would detain me.

It repenteth me not that my summons doth ride upon the blasting winds which multiply the sting of my bitterness; And great black slimy shapes shall rise from brackish pits and vomit forth their pustulence into his (her) puny brain.

I call upon the messengers of doom to slash with grim delight this victim I hath chosen. Silent is that voiceless bird that feeds upon the brain-pulp of him (her) who hath tormented me, and the agony of the is to be shall sustain itself in shrieks of pain, only to serve as signals of warning to those who would resent my being.

Oh come forth in the name of Abaddon and destroy him (her) whose name I giveth as a sign.

Oh great brothers of the night, thou who makest my place of comfort, who rideth out upon the hot winds of Hell, who dwelleth in the devil's fane; Move and appear! Present yourselves to him (her) who sustaineth the rottenness of the mind that moves the gibbering mouth that mocks the just and strong!; rend that gaggling tongue and close his (her) throat, Oh Kali! Pierce his (her) lungs with the stings of scorpions. Oh Sekhmet!

Plunge his (her) substance into the dismal void, Oh mighty Dagon!

I thrust aloft the bifid barb of Hell and on its tines resplendently impaled my sacrifice through vengeance rests!

Shemhamforash!   Hail Satan!

INVOCATION EMPLOYED TOWARDS
THE CONJURATION OF COMPASSION

WITH the anger of anguish and the wrath of the stifled, I pour forth my voices, wrapped in rolling thunder, that you may hear!

Oh great lurkers in the darkness, oh guardians of the way, oh minions of the might of Thoth! Move and appear! Present yourselves to us in your benign power, in behalf of one who believes and is stricken with torment.

Isolate him in the bulwark of your protection, for he is undeserving of anguish and desires it not.

Let that which bears against him be rendered powerless and devoid of substance.

Succor him through fire and water, earth and air, to regain what he has lost.

Strengthen with fire the marrow of our friend and companion, our comrade of the Left-Hand Path.

Through the power of Satan let the earth and its pleasures re-enter his being.

Allow his vital saltes to flow unhampered, that he may savor the carnal nectars of his future desires.

Strike dumb his adversary, formed or formless, that he may emerge joyful and strong from that which afflicts him.

Allow no misfortune to allay his path, for he is of us, and therefore to be cherished.

Restore him to power, to joy, to unending dominion over the reverses that have beset him.

Build around and within him the exultant radiance that will herald his emergence from the stagnant morass which engulfs him.

This we command, in the name of Satan, whose mercies flourish and whose sustenance will prevail!

As Satan reigns so shall his own whose name is as this sound: (name) is the vessel whose flesh is as the earth; life everlasting, world without end!

Shemhamforash! Hail Satan!

THE ENOCHIAN KEYS

THE ENOCHIAN LANGUAGE
AND THE ENOCHIAN KEYS

THE magical language used in Satanic ritual is Enochian, a language thought to be older than Sanskrit, with a sound grammatical and syntactical basis. It resembles Arabic in some sounds and Hebrew and Latin in others. It first appeared in print in 1659 in a biography of John Dee, the famous Sixteenth Century seer and court astrologer. This work, by Meric Casaubon, describes the occultist Dee's activities with his associate, Edward Kelly, in the art of scrying or crystal gazing.

Instead of the usual crystal ball, Kelly, who was the gazer, used a many-faceted trapezohedron. The "angels" referred to in Kelly's first revelation of the Enochian Keys, obtained through the windows of the crystal, are only "angels" because occultists to this day have lain ill with metaphysical constipation. Now the crystal clears, and the "angels" are seen as "angles" and the windows to the fourth dimension are thrown open—and to the frightened, the Gates of Hell.

I have presented my translation of the following calls with an archaic but Satanically correct unvarnishing of the translation employed by the Order of the Golden Dawn in the late Nineteenth Century. In Enochian the meaning of the words, combined with the quality of the words, unite to create a pattern of sound which can cause tremendous reaction in the atmosphere. The barbaric tonal qualities of this language give it a truly magical effect which cannot be described.

155

For many years the Enochian Keys, or Calls, have been shrouded in secrecy. The few printings that have existed completely eliminate the correct wording, as the proper translation has been disguised through the use of euphemisms, and only designed to throw the inept magician and/or would-be inquisitor off the track. Apocryphal as they have become (and who can tell what grim reality provokes the "fantasy"), the Enochian Calls are the Satanic paeans of faith. Dispensing with such once-pragmatic whitewashing in terms such as "holy" and "angelic," and arbitrarily chosen groups of numbers, the purpose of which were only to act as substitutes for "blasphemous" words—here, then, are the TRUE Enochian Calls, as received from an unknown hand.*

---

* The unexpurgated version, translated by Anton LaVey.

THE FIRST KEY

The First Enochian Key represents an initial proclamation from Satan, stating the inception of the laws of temporal theologies and of the lasting power which resides in those bold enough to recognize earthly beginnings and absolutes.

THE FIRST KEY
(Enochian)

Ol sonuf vaoresaji, gohu IAD Balata, elanusaha caelazod: sobrazod-ol Roray i ta nazodapesad, Giraa ta maelpereji, das hoel-qo qaa notahoa zodimezod, od comemahe ta nobeloha zodien; soba tahil ginonupe pereje aladi, das vaurebes obolehe giresam. Casarem ohorela caba Pire: das zodonurenusagi cab: erem Iadanahe. Pilahe farezodem zodenurezoda adana gono Iadapiel das home-tohe: soba ipame lu ipamis: das sobolo vepe zodomeda poamal, od bogira aai ta piape Piamoel od Vaoan! Zodacare, eca, od zodameranu! odo cicale Qaa; zodoreje, lape zodiredo Noco Mada, hoathahe Saitan!

THE FIRST KEY
(English)

I reign over thee, saith the Lord of the Earth, in power exalted above and below, in whose hands the sun is a glittering sword and the moon a through-thrusting fire, who measureth your garments in the midst of my vestures, and trusseth you up as the palms of my hands, and brightened your vestments with Infernal light.

I made ye a law to govern the holy ones, and delivered a rod with wisdom supreme. You lifted your voices and swore your allegiance to Him that liveth triumphant, whose beginning is not, nor end cannot be, which shineth as a flame in the midst of your palaces, and reigneth amongst you as the balance of life!

Move therefore, and appear! Open the mysteries of your creation! Be friendly unto me, for I am the same!—the true worshipper of the highest and ineffable King of Hell!

THE SECOND KEY

In order to pay homage to the very lusts which sustain the continuance of life, itself, The Second Enochian Key extends this recognition of our earthly heritage unto a talisman of power.

THE SECOND KEY
(Enochian)

Adagita vau-pa-ahe zodonugonu fa-a-ipe salada! Vi-i-vau el! Sobame ial-pereji i-zoda-zodazod pi-adapehe casarema aberameji ta ta-labo paracaleda qo-ta lores-el-qo turebesa ooge balatohe! Giui cahisa lusada oreri od micalapape cahisa bia ozodonugonu! lape noanu tarofe coresa tage o-quo maninu IA-I-DON. Torezodu! gohe-el, zodacare eca ca-no-quoda! zodameranu micalazodo od ozadazodame vaurelar; lape zodir IOIAD!

THE SECOND KEY
(English)

Can the wings of the winds hear your voices of wonder?;
O you!, the great spawn of the worms of the Earth!, whom the
Hell fire frames in the depth of my jaws!, whom I have prepared as cups for a wedding or as flowers regaling the cham-
bers of lust!

Stronger are your feet than the barren stone! Mightier are
your voices than the manifold winds! For you are become as a
building such as is not, save in the mind of the All-Powerful
manifestation of Satan!

Arise!, saith the First! Move therefore unto his servants!
Show yourselves in power, and make me a strong seer-of-things,
for I am of Him that liveth forever!

THE THIRD KEY

The Third Enochian Key establishes the leadership of the earth upon the hands of those great Satanic magicians who throughout the successive ages have held dominion over the peoples of the world.

THE THIRD KEY
(Enochian)

Micama! goho Pe-IAD! zodir com-selahe azodien biabe os-lon-dohe. Norezodacahisa otahila Gigipahe; vaunud-el-cahisa ta-pu-ime qo-mos-pelehe telocahe; qui-i-inu toltoregi cahisa i cahisaji em ozodien; dasata beregida od torezodul! Ili e-Ol balazodareji, od aala tahilanu-os netaabe: daluga vaomesareji elonusa cape-mi-ali varoesa *cala* homila; cocasabe fafenu izodizodope, od miinoagi de ginetaabe: vaunu na-na-e-el: panupire malapireji caosaji. Pilada noanu vaunalahe balata od-vaoan. Do-o-i-ape mada: goholore, gohus, amiranu! Micama! Yehusozod ca-ca-com, od do-o-a-inu noari micaolazoda a-ai-om. Casarameji gohia: Zodacare! Vaunigilaji! od im-ua-mar pugo pelapeli Ananael Qo-a-an.

THE THIRD KEY
(English)

Behold!, saith Satan, I am a circle on whose hands stand the Twelve Kingdoms. Six are the seats of living breath, the rest are as sharp sickles, or the Horns of Death. Therein the creatures of Earth are and are not, except in mine own hands which sleep and shall rise!

In the first I made ye stewards and placed ye in the Twelve seats of government, giving unto every one of you power successively over the Nine true ages of time, so that from the highest vessels and the corners of your governments you might work my power, pouring down the fires of life and increase continually on the Earth. Thus you are become the skirts of justice and truth. In Satan's name, rise up! Show yourselves! Behold!, his mercies flourish, and his name is become mighty among us. In whom we say: Move!, Ascend!, and apply yourselves unto us as the partakers of His secret wisdom in your creation!

THE FOURTH KEY

The Fourth Enochian Key refers to the cycling
of the ages of time.

THE FOURTH KEY
(Enochian)

Otahil elasadi babaje, od dorepaha gohol: gi-cahisaje auauago coremepe *peda*, dasonuf vi-vau-di-vau? Casaremi oeli *meapeme* sobame agi coremepo carep-el: casaremeji caro-o-dazodi cahisa od vaugeji; dasata ca-pi-mali cahisa ca-pi-ma-on: od elonusahinu cahisa ta el-o *calaa*. Torezodu nor-quasahi od fe-caosaga: Bagile zodir e-na-IAD: das iod apila! Do-o-a-ipe quo-A-AL, zodacare! Zodameranu obelisonugi resat-el aaf nor-mo-lapi!

THE FOURTH KEY
(English)

I have set my feet in the South, and have looked about me, saying: Are not the thunders of increase those which reign in the second angle?

Under whom I have placed those whom none hath yet numbered, but One; in whom the second beginnings of things are and wax strong, successively adding the numbers of time, and their powers doth stand as the first of the nine!

Arise!, you sons of pleasure, and visit the Earth; for I am the Lord, your God, which is and liveth forever!

In the name of Satan, Move!, and show yourselves as pleasant deliverers, that you may praise Him among the sons of men!

THE FIFTH KEY

The Fifth Enochian Key affirms the Satanic placing of traditional priests and wizards upon the earth for the purpose of misdirection.

THE FIFTH KEY
(Enochian)

Sapahe zodimii du-i-be, od noasa ta qu-a-nis, adarocahe dorepehal caosagi od faonutas peripesol ta-be-liore. Casareme A-me-ipezodi na-zodaretahe *afa;* od dalugare zodizodope zodelida caosaji tol-toregi; od zod-cahisa esiasacahe El ta-vi-vau; od iao-d tahilada das hubare *pe-o-al;* soba coremefa cahisa ta Ela Vaulasa od Quo-Co-Casabe. Eca niisa od darebesa quo-a-asa: fetahe-ar-ezodi od beliora: ia-ial eda-nasa cicalesa; bagile Ge-iad I-el!

THE FIFTH KEY
(English)

The mighty sounds have entered into the third angle and are become as seedlings of folly, smiling with contempt upon the Earth, and dwelling in the brightness of the Heaven as continual comforters to the destroyers of self.

Unto whom I fastened the pillars of gladness, the lords of the righteous, and gave them vessels to water the earth with her creatures. They are the brothers of the First and the Second, and the beginning of their own seats which are garnished with myriad ever-burning lamps, whose numbers are as the First, the ends, and the contents of time!

Therefore, come ye and obey your creation. Visit us in peace and comfort. Conclude us receivers of your mysteries; for why? Our Lord and Master is the All-One!

THE SIXTH KEY

The Sixth Enochian Key establishes the structure and form of that which has become the Order of the Trapezoid and Church of Satan.

THE SIXTH KEY
(Enochian)

Gahe sa-div cahisa *em*, micalazoda Pil-zodinu, sobam El haraji mir babalonu od obeloce samevelaji, dalagare malapereji ar-caosaji od *acame* canale, sobola zodare fa-beliareda caosaji od cahisa aneta-na miame ta Viv od Da. Daresare Sol-petahe-bienu. Be-ri-ta od zodacame ji-mi-calazodo: sob-ha-atahe tarianu luia-he od ecarinu MADA Qu-a-a-on!

THE SIXTH KEY
(English)

The spirits of the fourth angle are Nine, mighty in the trapezoid, whom the first hath formed, a torment to the wretched and a garland to the wicked; giving unto them fiery darts to vanne the earth, and Nine continual workmen whose courses visit with comfort the Earth, and are in government and continuance as the Second and Third.

Therefore, harken unto my voice! I have talked of you, and I move you in power and presence, whose works shall be a song of honor, and the praise of your God in your creation!

THE SEVENTH KEY

The Seventh Enochian Key is used to invoke lust, pay homage to glamor, and rejoice in the delights of the flesh.

THE SEVENTH KEY
(Enochian)

Ra-asa isaiamanu para-di-zoda oe-cari-mi aao iala-pire-gahe Quí-inu. Enai butamonu od inoasa *ni* pa-ra-diala. Casaremeji ujeare cahirelanu, od zodonace lucifatianu, caresa ta vavale-zodirenu tol-hami. Soba lonudohe od ñuame cahisa ta Da o Desa vo-ma-dea od pi-beliare itahila rita od miame ca-ni-quola rita! Zodacare! Zodameranu! Iecarimi Quo-a-dahe od I-mica-ol-zododa aaiome. Bajirele papenore idalugama elonusahi-od umapelifa vau-ge-ji Bijil—IAD!

THE SEVENTH KEY
(English)

The East is a house of harlots singing praises among the flames of the first glory wherein the Dark Lord hath opened His mouth; and they are become as living dwellings in whom the strength of man rejoiceth; and they are appareled with ornaments of brightness, such as work wonders on all creatures. Whose kingdoms and continuance are as the Third and Fourth, strong towers and places of comfort, the seats of pleasure and continuance. O ye servants of pleasure, Move!, Appear!, sing praises unto the Earth and be mighty amongst us. For that to this remembrance is given power, and our strength waxeth strong in our comforter.

THE EIGHTH KEY

The Eighth Enochian Key refers to the emergence of the Satanic Age.

THE EIGHTH KEY
(Enochian)

Bazodemelo i ta pi-ripesonu olanu Na-zodavabebe *ox*.
Casaremeji varanu cahisa vaugeji asa berameji balatoha: goho
IAD. Soba miame tarianu ta lolacis Abaivoninu od azodiajiere
riore. Irejila cahisa da das pa-aox busada Caosago, das cahisa
od ipuranu telocahe cacureji o-isalamahe lonucaho od Vovina
carebafe? NIISO! bagile avavago gohon. NIISO! bagile mamao
siaionu, od mabezoda IAD oi asa-momare poilape. NIIASA!
Zodameranu ciaosi caosago od belioresa od coresi ta a beramiji.

THE EIGHTH KEY
(English)

The midday of the first is as the third indulgence made of hyacinthine pillars, in whom the elders are become strong, which I have prepared for mine own justice, saith Satan, whose long continuance shall be as bucklers to Leviathan. How many are there which remain in the glory of the earth, which are, and shall not see death until the house falls and the dragon doth sink? Rejoice!, for the crowns of the temple and the robe of Him that is, was, and shall be crowned are no longer divided! Come forth!, Appear!, to the terror of the Earth, and to the comfort of such as are prepared!

THE NINTH KEY

The Ninth Enochian Key warns of the use of substances, devices or pharmaceuticals which might lead to the delusion and subsequent enslavement of the master. A protection against false values.

THE NINTH KEY
(Enochian)

Micaoli beranusaji perejela napeta ialapore, das barinu efafaje *Pe* vaunupeho olani od obezoda, soba-ca upaahe cahisa tatanu od tarananu balie, alare busada so-bolunu od cahisa hoel-qo ca-no-quodi *cial*. Vaunesa aladonu mom caosago ta iasa olalore gianai limelala. Amema cahisa sobra madarida zod cahisa! Ooa moanu cahisa avini darilapi caosajinu: od butamoni pareme zodumebi canilu. Dazodisa etahamezoda cahisa dao, od mireka ozodola cahisa pidiai Colalala. Ul ci ninu a sobame ucime. Bajile? IAD BALATOHE cahirelanu pare! NIISO! od upe ofafafe; bajile a-cocasahe icoresaka a uniji beliore.

THE NINTH KEY
(English)

A mighty guard of fire with two-edged swords flaming (which contain the vials of delusion, whose wings are of wormwood and of the marrow of salt), have set their feet in the West, and are measured with their ministers. These gather up the moss of the Earth, as the rich man doth his treasure. Cursed are they whose iniquities they are! In their eyes are millstones greater than the Earth, and from their mouths run seas of blood. Their brains are covered with diamonds, and upon their heads are marble stones. Happy is he on whom they frown not. For Why? The Lord of Righteousness rejoiceth in them! Come away, and leave your vials, for the time is such as requireth comfort!

THE TENTH KEY

The Tenth Enochian Key creates rampant wrath and produces violence. Dangerous to employ unless one has learnt to safeguard his own immunity; a random lightning bolt!

THE TENTH KEY
(Enochian)

Coraxo cahisa coremepe, od belanusa Lucala azodiazodore paebe Soba iisononu cahisa uirequo *ope* copehanu od racalire maasi bajile caosagi; das yalaponu dosiji od basajime; od ox ex dazodisa siatarisa od salaberoxa cynuxire faboanu. Vaunala cahisa conusata das *daox* cocasa ol Oanio yore vohima ol jizod-yazoda od eoresa cocasaji pelosi molui das pajeipe, laraji same darolanu matorebe cocasaji emena. El pataralaxa yolaci matabe nomiji mononusa olora jinayo anujelareda. Ohyo! ohyo! noibe Ohyo! caosagonu! Bajile madarida i zodirope cahiso darisapa! NIISO! caripe ipe nidali!

THE TENTH KEY
(English)

The thunders of wrath doth slumber in the North, in the likeness of an oak whose branches are dung-filled nests of lamentation and weeping laid up for the Earth, which burn night and day and vomit out the heads of scorpions and live sulphur mingled with poison. These be the thunders that in an instant roar with a hundred mighty earthquakes and a thousand as many surges, which rest not, nor know any time here. One rock bringeth forth a thousand, even as the heart of man doth his thoughts. Woe! Woe!, Yea!, woe be to the Earth, for her iniquity is, was, and shall be great. Come away! But not your mighty sounds!

THE ELEVENTH KEY

The Eleventh Enochian Key is used to herald the coming of the dead and establish a sustenance beyond the grave. To bind to the earth. A funerary call.

THE ELEVENTH KEY
(Enochian)

Oxiayala holado, od zodirome O coraxo das zodiladare raasyo. Od vabezodire cameliaxa od bahala: NIISO! salamanu telocahe! Casaremanu hoel-qo, od ti ta zod cahisa soba coremefa i ga. NIISA! bagile aberameji nonuçape. Zodacare eca od Zodameranu! odo cicale Qaa! Zodoreje, lape zodiredo Noco Mada, hoathahe Saitan!

THE ELEVENTH KEY
(English)

The mighty throne growled and there were five thunders that flew into the East. And the eagle spake and cried aloud: Come away from the house of death! And they gathered themselves together and became those of whom it measured, and they are the deathless ones who ride the whirlwinds. Come away! For I have prepared a place for you. Move therefore, and show yourselves! Unveil the mysteries of your creation. Be friendly unto me, for I am your God, the true worshipper of the flesh that liveth forever!

THE TWELFTH KEY

The Twelfth Enochian Key is used to vent one's displeasure towards man's need for misery, and bring forth torment and conflict to the harbingers of woe.

THE TWELFTH KEY
(Enochian)

Nonuci dasonuf Babaje od cahisa *ob* hubaio tibibipe?
alalare ataraahe od ef! Darix fafenu *mianu* ar Enayo ovof!
Soba dooainu aai i VONUPEHE. Zodacare, gohusa, od
Zodameranu. Odo cicale Qaa! Zodoreje, lape zodiredo Noco
Mada, hoathahe Saitan!

THE TWELFTH KEY
(English)

O ye that range in the South and are the lanterns of sorrow, buckle your armour and visit us! Bring forth the legions of the army of Hell, that the Lord of the Abyss may be magnified, whose name amongst ye is Wrath! Move therefore, and appear! Open the mysteries of your creation! Be friendly unto me, for I am the same!, the true worshipper of the highest and ineffable King of Hell!

THE THIRTEENTH KEY

The Thirteenth Enochian Key is used to make the sterile lustful and vex those who would deny the pleasures of sex.

THE THIRTEENTH KEY
(Enochian)

Napeai Babajehe das berinu *vax* ooaona latinuji vonupehe doalime: conisa olalogi oresaha das cahisa afefa. Micama isaro Mada od Lonu-sahi-toxa, das ivaumeda aai Jirosabe. Zodacare od Zodameranu. Odo cicale Qaa! Zodoreje, lape zodiredo Noco Mada, hoathahe Saitan!

THE THIRTEENTH KEY
(English)

O ye swords of the South, which have eyes to stir up the wrath of sin, making men drunken which are empty; Behold! the promise of Satan and His power, which is called amongst ye a bitter sting! Move and appear! Unveil the mysteries of your creation! For I am the servant of the same, your God, the true worshipper of the highest and ineffable King of Hell!

THE FOURTEENTH KEY

The Fourteenth Enochian Key is a call for vengeance and the manifestation of justice.

THE FOURTEENTH KEY
(Enochian)

Noroni bajihie pasahasa Oiada! das tarinuta mireca *ol* tahila dodasa tolahame caosago *h*omida: das berinu orocahe *quare*: Micama! Bial! Oiad; aisaro toxa das ivame aai Balatima. Zodacare od Zodameranu! Od cicale Qaa! Zodoreje, lape zodiredo Noco Mada, hoathahe Saitan!

THE FOURTEENTH KEY
(English)

O ye sons and daughters of mildewed minds, that sit in judgment of the iniquities wrought upon me—Behold! the voice of Satan; the promise of Him who is called amongst ye the accuser and supreme tribune! Move therefore, and appear! Open the mysteries of your creation! Be friendly unto me, for I am the same!, the true worshipper of the highest and ineffable King of Hell!

THE FIFTEENTH KEY.

The Fifteenth Enochian Key is a resolution of acceptance and understanding of the masters whose duty lies in administering to the seekers after spiritual gods.

THE FIFTEENTH KEY
(Enochian)

Ilasa! tabaanu li-El pereta, casaremanu upaahi cahisa *dareji;* das oado caosaji oresacore: das omaxa monasaçi Baeouibe od emetajisa Iaiadix. Zodacare od Zodameranu! Odo cicale Qaa. Zodoreje, lape zodiredo Noco Mada, hoathahe Saitan!

THE FIFTEENTH KEY
(English).

O thou, the governor of the first flame, under whose wings are the spinners of cobwebs that weave the Earth with dryness; that knowest the great name "righteousness" and the seal of false honor. Move therefore, and appear! Open the mysteries of your creation! Be friendly unto me, for I am the same!, the true worshipper of the highest and ineffable King of Hell!

THE SIXTEENTH KEY.

The Sixteenth Enochian Key gives recognition of the wondrous contrasts of the earth, and of the sustenance of these dichotomies.

THE SIXTEENTH KEY
(Enochian)

Ilasa viviala pereta! Salamanu balata, das acaro odazodi busada, od belioraxa balita: das inusi caosaji lusadanu *emoda*: das ome od taliobe: darilapa iehe ilasa Mada Zodilodarepe. Zodacare od Zodameranu. Odo cicale Qaa: zodoreje, lape zodiredo Noco Mada, hoathahe Saitan!

THE SIXTEENTH KEY
(English)

O thou second flame, the house of justice, which hast thy beginnings in glory and shalt comfort the just; which walketh upon the Earth with feet of fire; which understands and separates creatures! Great art thou in the God of stretch-forth-and-conquer. Move therefore, and appear! Open the mysteries of your creation! Be friendly unto me, for I am the same!, the true worshipper of the highest and ineffable King of Hell!

THE SEVENTEENTH KEY
(English)

THE SEVENTEENTH KEY

The Seventeenth Enochian Key is used to enlighten the benumbed and destroy through revelation.

THE SEVENTEENTH KEY
(Enochian)

Ilasa dial pereta! soba vaupaahe cahisa nanuba zodixalayo dodasihe od berinuta *faxisa* hubaro tasataxa yolasa: soba Iad *i* Vonupehe o Uonupehe: aladonu dax ila od toatare! Zodacare od Zodameranu! Odo cicale Qaa! Zodoreje, lape zodiredo Noco Mada, hoathahe Saitan!

THE SEVENTEENTH KEY
(English)

O thou third flame!, whose wings are thorns to stir up vexation, and who hast myriad living lamps going before thee; whose God is wrath in anger—Gird up thy loins and harken! Move therefore, and appear! Open the mysteries of your creation! Be friendly unto me, for I am the same!, the true worshipper of the highest and ineffable King of Hell!

THE SEVENTEENTH KEY
(English)

THE EIGHTEENTH KEY

The Eighteenth Enochian Key opens the gates of Hell and casts up Lucifer and his blessing.

THE EIGHTEENTH KEY
(Enochian)

Ilasa micalazoda olapireta ialpereji beliore: das odo
Busadire Oiad ouoaresa caosago: casaremeji Laiada *eranu*
berinutasa cafafame das ivemeda aqoso adoho Moz, od maof-
fasa. Bolape como belioreta pamebeta. Zodacare od Zodameranu! Odo cicale Qaa. Zodoreje, lape zodiredo Noco Mada,
hoathahe Saitan!

THE EIGHTEENTH KEY
(English)

O thou mighty light and burning flame of comfort!, that unveilest the glory of Satan to the center of the Earth; in whom the great secrets of truth have their abiding; that is called in thy kingdom: "strength through joy," and is not to be measured. Be thou a window of comfort unto me. Move therefore, and appear! Open the mysteries of your creation! Be friendly unto me, for I am the same!, the true worshipper of the highest and ineffable King of Hell!

THE NINETEENTH KEY

The Nineteenth Enochian Key is the great sustainer of the natural balance of the earth, the law of thrift, and of the jungle. It lays bare all hypocrisy and the sanctimonious shall become as slaves under it. It brings forth the greatest outpouring of wrath upon the miserable, and lays the foundation of success for the lover of life.

THE NINETEENTH KEY
(Enochian)

Madariatza das perifa LIL cahisa micaolazoda saanire caosago od fifisa balzodizodarasa Iaida. Nonuca gohulime: Micama adoianu MADA faoda beliorebe, soba ooaona cahisa luciftias peripesol, das aberaasasa nonucafe netaaibe caosaji od tilabe adapehaheta damepelozoda, tooata nonucafe jimicalazodoma larasada tofejilo marebe yareyo IDOIGO, od torezodulape yaodafe gohola, Caosaga, tabaoreda saanire, od caharisateosa yorepoila tiobela busadire, tilabe noalanu paida oresaba, od dodaremeni zodayolana. Elazodape tilaba paremeji peripesatza, od ta qurelesata booapisa. Lanibame oucaho sayomepe, od caharisateosa ajitoltorenu, mireca qo tiobela lela. Tonu paomebeda dizodalamo asa pianu, od caharisateosa aji-la-tore-torenu paracahe a sayomepe. Coredazodizoda dodapala od fifalazoda, lasa manada, od faregita bamesa omaosa. Conisabera od auauotza tonuji oresa; catabela noasami tabejesa leuitahemonuji. Vanucahi omepetilabe oresa! Bagile? Moooabe OL coredazodizoda. El capimao itzomatzipe, od cacocasabe gosaa. Bajilęnu pii tianuta a babalanuda, od faoregita teloca uo uime.

Madariatza, torezodu !!! Oadariatza orocaha aboaperi! Tabaori periazoda aretabasa! Adarepanu coresata dobitza! Yolacame periazodi arecoazodiore, od quasabe qotinuji! Ripire

269

paaotzata sagacore! Umela od peredazodare cacareji Aoiveae coremepeta! Torezodu! Zodacare od Zodameranu, asapeta sibesi butamona das surezodasa Tia balatanu. Odo cicale Qaa₂ od Ozodazodama pelapeli IADANAMADA!

THE NINETEENTH KEY
(English)

O ye pleasures which dwell in the first air, ye are mighty in the parts of the Earth, and execute the judgment of the mighty. Unto you it is said: Behold the face of Satan, the beginning of comfort, whose eyes are the brightness of the stars, which provided you for the government of the Earth, and her unspeakable variety; furnishing you a power of understanding to dispose all things according to the providence of Him that sitteth on the Infernal Throne, and rose up in the Beginning saying: The Earth, let her be governed by her parts; and let there be division in her; the glory of her may be always drunken and vexed in itself. Her course, let it run with the fulfillment of lust; and as an handmaiden, let her serve them. One season, let it confound another; and let there be no creature upon or within her the same. All her numbers, let them differ in their qualities; and let there be no one creature equal with another. The reasonable creatures of the Earth, and Men, let them vex and weed out one another; and their dwelling places, let them forget their names. The work of Man and his pomp, let them be defaced. His buildings, let them become caves for the beasts of the field! Confound her understanding with darkness! For why? it repenteth me that I have made Man. One while let her be known, and another while a stranger; because she is the bed of a harlot, and the dwelling place of Lucifer the King.

Open wide the gates of Hell! The lower heavens beneath you, let them serve you! Govern those who govern! Cast down such as fall. Bring forth those that increase, and destroy the rotten. No place, let it remain in one number. Add and diminish until the stars be numbered. Arise! Move! and appear before the covenant of His mouth, which He hath sworn unto us in His justice. Open the mysteries of your creation, and make us partakers of the UNDEFILED WISDOM.

YANKEE ROSE